CHARLIE'S BOYS

CHARLIE'S BOYS

AJAY JAIN

HARPER
VANTAGE

HarperCollins *Publishers* India

First published in India by HarperVantage 2025
An imprint of HarperCollins *Publishers*
HarperCollins *Publishers* India, Cyber City,
Building 10-A, Gurugram, Haryana – 122002, India
www.harpercollins.co.in

2 4 6 8 10 9 7 5 3 1

Copyright © Ajay Jain 2025

P-ISBN: 978-93-7307-115-2
E-ISBN: 978-93-7307-354-5

The views and opinions expressed in this book are the author's own and the facts are as reported by him/her, and the publishers are not in any way liable for the same.

Some names and identifying details have been changed to protect the privacy of individuals.

Ajay Jain asserts the moral right
to be identified as the author of this work.

All rights reserved. No part of this publication may be reproduced, stored in a retrieval system, or transmitted, in any form or by any means, electronic, mechanical, photocopying, recording or otherwise, without the prior permission of the publishers.

Without limiting the exclusive rights of any author, contributor or the publisher of this publication, any unauthorized use of this publication to train generative artificial intelligence (AI) technologies is expressly prohibited. HarperCollins also exercise their rights under Article 4(3) of the Digital Single Market Directive 2019/790 and expressly reserve this publication from the text and data-mining exception.

Typeset in 11.5pt/15 Adobe Garamond Pro
by HarperCollins *Publishers* India Pvt. Ltd

Printed and bound at
Thomson Press (India) Ltd

This book is produced from independently certified FSC® paper
to ensure responsible forest management.

*

HarperCollins *Publishers*, Macken House, 39/40 Mayor Street Upper, Dublin 1, D01 C9W8, Ireland

THE SCHOOL MOTTO

Sapere Aude, Sincere et Constanter
Dare to be Wise, Sincere and Constant

BACK TO SCHOOL – FIGHTING TEARS!

Tears.
Of apprehension when I entered St. Columba's School for the first time as a five-year-old.
Tears.
Of a yearning when I visited fifty years later.
While I left the school, the school never left me. It was still there, waiting, with little changed. The buildings, the classrooms, the fields, the canteen—they were the same. As was the lighting in the corridors, the water in the coolers and the odour from the bathrooms. Weathering the test of time were the murals on the walls, the stone on the floor, the banisters on the stairs and the bricks in the walls. The doors to classrooms were their robust self, their aluminium latches still intact; iron-framed windows open as always, for nature to provide its air-conditioning.

Of course, it was a different era. Then and now. As I walked the corridors, I expected a certain Br D'Souza, a Mrs Kak, a Mr Rocha to appear, requiring me to wish them a good morning or a good afternoon and their nods of acknowledgement. My ears were cocked for the Walter's bell to make it to class on time, lest Charlie get upset. Oh Walter, all of us groaned when your dong marked the end of the lunch break; it's ring would now be music to the ears, if only I could hear it just one more time.

I imagined walking into any of the classrooms, finding my desk, unlocking it, taking the ink pot and filling the fountain pen. And listening. To the mute walls, the boisterous students and the stern teachers. The lectures will be the same, but the lessons won't.

And thus, this memoir. Where I retraced the same steps but arrived elsewhere. The past was a metamorphosis. Revisiting it was one too. A certain 'me' emerged after thirteen formative years in the institution, the process of writing this journal shaped another 'me.'

Why I Wrote the Memoir

I was in St. Columba's High School from 1975 to 1988.

I wrote this memoir for myself. To pay an ode to the institution and its teachers.

To re-live the joy of childhood and adolescence. To revise the lessons learnt. To reconnect with my schoolmates. To remind myself of the innocence and simplicity of the times gone by.

To tell myself, life need not be very different than what it was in school. It is only a matter of the choices we make. So, we can hum along, free in the mind, nimble on our feet, light in the heart. It does not take much to be the same child in spirit as we were back then, ever the youth in appearance and outlook.

I wrote this memoir for you. So, you may pause a moment. Go back to your own school. And then experience the same sentiment, the same resurgence, the same catharsis I did.

So many people in school contributed to shaping who I am today. The most important thing they taught me? Pay it forward. So, the lamp of knowledge, of kindness, of goodness keeps burning.

I wrote this memoir lest I forget.

If I want my school to stay my inspiration, my anchor, my rock, my teacher, my family, my healer, then I must not forget. So, I wrote it all down—the events, the anecdotes, the impressions and the reflections. As I did, I sensed magic unfolding.

The more I wrote, more the doors opened. To secret passages, memories lining their walls. Each memory made me contemplative, triggering more, including those I thought I had no recollection of. I tried to re-live each in my mind, as vividly as possible. Was I learning something for the first time? Was I bonding with a new friend? Was I in a scuffle? Was I having fun? Was I playing a prank? Was I making someone proud of me, or was I embarrassing them?

When you stir memories, it is like placing a spool of film in a projector and flicking it on. Evoking nostalgia like nothing else can. I watched scenes play out in front of my eyes. Endlessly. And tangibly. Not in three dimensions, but four—add emotion to it. But the past is not something you can leave behind. What happened in school continues to shape me. There is no status-quo; it is as dynamic now as it was then.

The school never forgets, it never leaves us, never stops educating us. To get the most out of school, we had to show up in the classroom diligently. To continue getting more, one has to show up at the memory bank.

But memory is fickle and unreliable and needs to be recorded. Continually. Routinely. Religiously. When you do, you accumulate both principal and interest. Making you progressively wealthy in moments, history and your own oneness.

This memoir is written from my heart. Because we were schooled in a place of love.

Call me sappy.

I took my school admission, and the time spent there for granted. I itched to get it over with so I could explore the world beyond the school walls. And now I feel I should have never left. One of our batchmates, Merwyn Fernandes, entered school at the young age of five. He stayed on as a computer teacher after twelfth standard and is still there. It was his only school. It has been his only job.

If I could go back in time, there are so many things I would do differently. I would forge stronger bonds with the boys. Be more attentive to teachers. Involve myself in more social activities—making a mark on the stage or the sports field.

The dynamics of time, space, mass and energy do not allow us to turn the clock back. But penning the memoir has rekindled memories. Made me relive the thirteen years I spent there. Reinforced a bond I was not conscious of. It has been like losing a love and then regaining it. You realize its value, and you hold it dear, not letting it go this time.

All it takes is listening to one's heart.

Admissions Open to St. Columba's School
January 7, 1941

St. Columba's opened its doors on January 7, 1941. The records show thirty-two boys showed up: five Catholics, eighteen Hindus, eight Muslims and one Sikh, conspicuous in his purple turban. Classes started as numbers swelled gradually. The vast majority of pupils were the sons of government officials, genial and easy going, and were fonder of pleasure and amusement than studying, as per official accounts of the time. Homework and preparative work of any kind were things they abominated. 'Our teacher,' said one of the youths, 'impose a lot of homework and yet call themselves Christian Brothers.'

If the boys thought they could get away with this attitude, then they should have paid attention to the address by Rev. S. Mulligan, Archbishop of Delhi, on the official opening of the school:

'St. Columba's is a dream I have had since I came to India—a dream I feared I would not see come true in my day. I looked on it as a mere possibility but faith, trust in God and the courage of the Brothers have made it a reality in the shortest time possible. There it stands today, under our eyes—an ornament to our city, a monument to the educational zeal of the Irish Christian Brothers, a credit to the architect who designed it, to the contractor who executed the work and to the Brothers, who supervised and improvised its routine.

If you ask me why I turned to these Brothers when there was the question of St. Columba's. I have known these Brothers all my life. I have been a witness of the wonderful educational work they have been doing at home and abroad. They have won laurels in every phase of educational work from the kindergarten up to the university curriculum.

Somebody has said that a school is as good as its teachers. If that be so, then I can predict that this school of Delhi will be second to none in India. Long and thorough has been the training these Brothers have received in their own Institute, while they are heirs to a tradition of successful teaching, stretching back for a century and a half. They have sacrificed everything dear to human nature—bright prospects, lucrative position, many of the pleasures of life—in order to dedicate themselves unreservedly to the intellectual and moral training of the youth of the country where they happened to be.

Parents have a right to expect their children will be given, during the course of their training, the love and an appreciation of the spiritual values of life that lie beyond all thinking and all action—that lie at the very basis of civilised society. A young man may leave college a prize winner, a classical scholar, and may be able "to roll to bed with a Latin phrase and rise with a verse of Greek," but unless his mind is clean and his heart is pure, he is not a cultured man but a monstrosity that may become a danger to the state. He is without self-control and unable to stem the tide of passion, of rouse, a lethargic will to action, is without a sense of responsibility to conscience, society or God. To plan education for mere intellectual activity without regard to character training and conduct seems a pitiless cruelty and a heavy handicap to a boy in after life. Unless the whole soul of the boy be trained, it may easily become a dumping ground for the ugliest universal filth.

That aspect of education has never been overlooked by the Brothers who have charge of St. Columba's. They have been trained themselves in a severe school and have learnt to love their boys. They have by constant contact with their pupils learned to recognise all that is good and noble in their character and of assisting them to the highest ideal of life. Parents in committing their children to the care of the Brothers may rest assured that they will progress not only in knowledge but in goodness and all the domestic and social virtues irrespective of the religion they may profess. The Brothers are bound to stand before the boy as a model, a living example of what he hopes to become. He may forget in later life his Geography, History, Mathematics; that does not matter much provided he does not forget his master, forget the devotion, the care and sympathy shown to him by such a master.

Personal contact and the subtle influence exercised by good teachers will react on the mind of the boy and steady him amid the fluctuations and aberrations of modern life.

I have great pleasure in declaring St. Columba's school open and I pray that it may become a nursery of good, intelligent boys who will be able to fight their way through under the standards of Truth, Justice, Religion and Charity.'

SCHOOL COLOURS
School Blazer: India Green
Trousers (Winter): Worsted Grey Flannel
Trousers or Shorts (Summer): White
Shirt: White
Shoes: Black
Socks or Stockings (Winter): Dark grey
Socks (Summer): White
School Belt and Tie: India Green and Canary Yellow

I Enter St. Columba's School

January 6, 1975

I did kindergarten twice. Not because I was dim but because my mother was bright.

My father grew up in rural Punjab and Haryana in north India. My grandfather was a schoolteacher, and most conversations with the men at home were about grades in school. My father made it to the big city and secured a respectable government job only because he scored well in the classroom. For him, pursuing quality education was non-negotiable.

He had clarity about the "what" and my mother about the "where." It would be St. Columba's for her son and the adjoining Convent of Jesus and Mary School for her daughter. Only because her elder sister's children had studied in these schools too.

There was a hitch though: Columba's only admitted those over five, while most others took in a year younger. My mother saw it as only a matter of adjusting the clock by a year; I was sent to Air Force Bal Bharti School at four, and then to Columba's when I turned five. To repeat the grade.

And thus, thirty-four years after the first set of students entered St. Columba's in 1941, I did too. And found me a chair and table in KG-D.

Brothers Waited to Receive You at the School Gates

Where our parents left off, Brothers took over seamlessly continuing their love and care.

Every day—without fail—the principal and two headmasters would be standing at the three gates of the school, welcoming students with a smile. Each of us wishing them a 'Good morning, Brother', some touching their hand, continuing without breaking stride. So as not be late for assembly or the classroom. And using any spare minutes to go to the bathroom, make small talk or finish any pending homework.

Also greeting the students were the guards, the maintenance staff, the gardeners in their khakis. Smiling, grinning, effortlessly—proof of their fondness for everyone and everything Columba's. They looked at you as if they knew you by name, but how could they? Or maybe they did—it would be no surprise if they had developed superpowers in this school.

Incidentally, if you reached the gates and did not find a Brother waiting, you knew you were in trouble. Because you were late!

A security guard from an agency checks you in at the gate now. She is ever smiling, no less warm than her khaki-clad predecessors. And yet, you get a sense of her presence being temporary; the agency could send a replacement anytime. But the earlier staff seemed as permanent as pillars holding the buildings up; for students would come and go, but they would always be standing and waiting, to greet you with a smile and a grin.

Anish walks to KG-D
January 6, 1975

Anish Tawakley was admitted to section A, but he just picked up his bag and walked to section D instead. His name would be added to section D's attendance register. Just like that. He would stay in section D till the tenth grade.

Why did he move? He had spotted Mrs Ruby Aimond, the class teacher of section D, whom he recognized as a friend of his aunt. Drawn to the familiarity of her presence in a strange place, he sought refuge—as only a five-year-old would.

If he had not moved that day, he and I might not have gone on to become best friends.

The Trauma of Forgetting My Handkerchief
February 19, 1975

'I forgot my hanky.'

These were probably the earliest collection of words I remember uttering together when in kindergarten. We lived walking distance from the school and my father would drop me every morning. On that particular day, when we reached the gates of the school, I realized I had forgotten my handkerchief. My father, his frame towering over me, promised to drop it on his way to work. He had a benign look, but his mind must have been saying, 'Seriously, is that the only fuss left in this world?'

A few hours passed, and there was no papa with the hanky. I finally went up to Mrs Aimond, our class teacher, to tell her my father had not yet come with my hanky. Was I the first—and perhaps only—child ever to share such a problem with her? She assured me he would come, I just needed to wait patiently. I trusted her words.

I could barely take my eyes off the door, but my father never showed up. It was the most distressing day of my five years of existence. Only I know how I fought my tears back then. I threw a tantrum with my mother at home in the afternoon and whined when my father came back from work in the evening. He felt so sorry; he took out my handkerchief from his pocket. He had taken it but forgot to stop by at the school. I wonder if my mother planted it on him, whispering my distressed state in his ear at the door before I met him.

The handkerchief was important to me. Then. And now. I still do not leave home without a clean, ironed one in my pocket. It has been my security blanket all my life; more so because of my OCD about personal hygiene. On occasions—very, very rare indeed—when I do leave home without one, my day feels as disturbed as it did when I forgot to carry my hanky to class KG-D of St. Columba's School.

Touched Paper by Foot? Go to Hell!
April 17, 1975

'If you touch paper with your foot accidentally, you can ask for forgiveness, and you will be okay. If you do so deliberately, which you did, you will definitely go to hell!'

Prashant Jain and Varun Pawha had me nearly crying with their scaremongering. All because I had pushed a piece of paper on the ground with my shoe. They went on psyching me for the sin I had committed, painting gory scenarios and I believed them. It would take me days to get out of the trauma.

In India, it is considered inauspicious by many to touch any objects of learning and writing by foot. To this day, if I 'sin' like this—always inadvertently, never deliberately—I whisper a silent prayer to say sorry. With Prashant and Varun on my mind.

Hear Our Prayer, O God

The school magazine carried a prayer, a true reflection of where the school's heart lies:

Eternal God, Bless us all

Both teachers and boys who work together in St. Columba's School.

Enable us to do our duties as school boys that we may serve you,

Our Father, through the service we give to others.

Make us truthful, honest and obedient as child that we may become men,

Always ready to serve our country and all who live in it.

Hear our Prayer, God.

For ourselves and our companions that we may understand what we are taught and that

we may be grateful for what others do for us.

For our parents and teachers that they may do what is good for our future and that by their example we may become good citizens of India.

For the poor people of India who have neither food nor shelter,

That those in authority may be moved to treat them as children of God

Deserving of the necessities of life.

For those who govern the country that they may be guided by thee

To rule with justice and compassion.

For all the nations in the world, especially our own country, that people may live in peace and brotherly love and that all the money wasted on hatred and destruction may be used to lessen the suffering of the unfortunate.

Hear our Prayer, O God.

A State of Emergency Declared
June 26, 1975

There was no newspaper in the morning. The radio was on, the only possible source of news, if any. My father was continually on the phone or talking to the neighbourhood uncles who were frantically walking in and out of the house. The one word I heard multiple times was 'Emergency.' The nation officially heard about it from the Prime Minister herself via a radio broadcast at eight in the morning of June 26.

It was too big a word for me to know the meaning of, but I could sense something was amiss. While I understood bits back then, it would be years before I comprehended what the day was about. Prime Minister Indira Gandhi had declared a state of emergency in the country, citing internal disturbances. The High Court of Allahabad had declared her election to the Parliament in 1971 as invalid and the opposition parties had been rallying masses against her Government for well over a year. Her desire to stay in power was cited as the reason for her to suspend all civil liberties, interpreting the Constitution to justify her actions, even curtailing the courts' powers for those seeking fair trials.

Rumours and opinions abounded for days, not taking a break till the Emergency was lifted after twenty-one months. Political leaders, journalists, activists, civilians and anyone who was even remotely opposed to the Government were detained on specious grounds. The provisions of the Maintenance of Internal Security Act and the Defence of India Act were invoked. How many were taken in? Over 100,000 people, according to the Shah Commission set up by the Janata government after routing the Congress Party at the polls for the first time in independent India in 1977.

Why were there no newspapers? Power to their offices and printing presses had been cut off the night before Indira Gandhi made the announcement. All media was subject to pre-censorship; the pliant or the scared ones toed the Government line—but not the *Indian Express,* the newspaper we got at home. They published a blank editorial and front page on June 28 rather than give in to any unjustified show of authority.

As the days and months passed, a national joke became popular: Government services became more efficient during this period, with all employees reporting to work on time, and carrying out the tasks they were assigned to. Adults would call it the silver lining of what was seen as a cloud over our relatively young democracy.

New Principal: The Last of the Irish Brothers to Hold the Post
July 1, 1975

We got a new principal; Br R.B. Oman took over the position from Br J.N. Foley. He would be the last of the Irish Brothers to hold the post, before handing over the baton to Br J.B. Pinto after seven years. Call us blessed, our batch would be in St. Columba's during its best years with such statesmen at its helm. Change would come, but we would have graduated by then.

'Jailed' for Stealing Jamun
July 15, 1975

Caught for plucking fruit and confined to a room, we had no idea of the punishment which would follow.

Those who lived at a walking distance from school would usually get picked up by our maids and servants after dispersal; of course, some parents picked their children too. On this occasion, two maids, including ours, reached out to a tree outside the Sacred Heart Cathedral to pluck some jamun (java plum). They were apprehended by caretakers and taken away to an office block with two tiny boys in tow. I sat in the office with them, all fearful, expecting to be sent to jail. I imagined I would never see home again.

I sat there, my brain fuzzy, eyes brimming with the beginning of a waterfall as a tough talking man made much ado about a handful of fruit. Likely to have already been spoiled before anyone ate them or devoured by squirrels and birds. After what seemed like an eternity but could not have been more than a few minutes, we were let go.

The jamun had to left behind. I wonder, now, who ate them finally?

Four years after that incident, we would move to a house in Kaka Nagar with a mature jamun tree in the lawns. We enjoyed the sweetest of fruits every summer during our stay there. We did not reprimand anyone in the neighbourhood for helping themselves to Nature's bounty.

Prashant Jain: The Original Best Friend. For a Short While.

August 8, 1975

I was not going back to my house after school. But, instead, to Prashant Jain's— where my parents, too, would come over in the evening and take me back after dinner. The ritual would switch the following Friday, with him coming home to mine and his parents joining us for dinner. This routine was regularly repeated well into the first grade.

Prashant was my first best friend but mutual disinterest set in shortly. We didn't want to spend time with one another; the fickle six years old that we were. But our parents did not share our sentiment and stayed close friends all their lives.

Around the same time, I found more friends for my parents. I became pals with a neighbour; he was three and I was five. Our parents met, liked each other more than this boy and I did, and stayed best friends till a family situation created a chasm between them twenty years later.

Sholay Makes Amitabh Bachchan the Undisputed King of Bollywood
August 15, 1975

Independence Day marked the release of what continues to be regarded as one of the most successful and perfect film in Bollywood ever: *Sholay*. After a tepid start, it picked up momentum to catch the nation's fancy. Everyone saw it. In fact, my parents and their friends exchanged notes on how many times they had seen it.

It also established Amitabh Bachchan as the undisputed king of Hindi cinema. Although he had made powerful impressions as the angry young man in *Zanjeer* in 1973 and as the anti-hero in *Deewar* earlier the same year, there was no looking back after Sholay. He would rule the coming decade, building a following even gods would envy.

The other sensation of the year was *Julie*, controversial for going into taboo territory: pre-marital sex and delivering a child out of wedlock when the man does a disappearing act. *Jai Santoshi Maa*, an out and out religious film, became one of the highest grossers of the year, laying the marker for things to come in the country.

'Stole' My Aunt's Hospital Money
December 3, 1975

Mrs Aimond found money on me, far more than what a kindergarten student should have on him. My parents were called.

An aunt had come visiting the previous day. My mother and her were sunbathing and my aunt's money had accidentally spilled on the cot they were sitting on. With their backs to it, I picked up a few notes and kept them in my school bag. Only to be spotted by the class teacher the following day.

The money was returned to the aunt of course, none of it spent or misplaced thankfully. She had gone to the hospital after meeting us and had been distraught when the time to pay the bills came; she had assumed she lost the money in the public bus on the way. Her elation to learn she had not, saved me from corporal punishment at home!

Mrs Ruby Aimond Did Not Move Out of KG-D for Decades

It could very well be a record of sorts.

When I graduated in 1988, Mrs Ruby Aimond was still in charge of KG-D. Even the location of the room had not changed. Turns out, she did not move out of those four walls throughout the decades she taught in St. Columba's. I doubt there has been any other teacher who could claim such a unique distinction.

Entered Class One
January 5, 1976

A new year and a new class, 1-D to be precise. Mrs M. Robinson was our class teacher. Not to be confused with the Miss Robinson who would join school years later, causing many a heart—of male teachers and students—to swoon!

How Do I Get a Haircut on Tuesdays?
March 9, 1976

'Your hair is too long. Do not come to class tomorrow without getting a cut.'

Mrs Robinson's warning left me stressed. Not because I had to cut my hair, but because it was a Tuesday. My mother was one of the millions in India who considered it inauspicious to cut hair on a Tuesday. So? How was I supposed to get one?

Of course, I did not. I was stressed all Tuesday and on Wednesday while heading to school. I tried to keep a low profile; praying to not be called up to explain why instructions were not followed. I kept dabbing my hair with my hands, as if they would suddenly appear shorter. Fortunately, Mrs Robinson did not notice me at all. I reached home and dragged my mother out to Andre's, the barber shop in the nearby Sunder Nagar market, in the middle of the afternoon to destress.

Somehow, I always got pulled up for long hair on Tuesdays more than any other days. I could not explain the reason for needing an additional day for fear of sounding ridiculous. Then, one day, I heard Saeed-ul-Islam, a classmate, say something when he was told to get a cut on a Tuesday: 'I will do it tomorrow since all barbers are closed on Tuesday.' The teacher understood and excused him. I had found my counterargument finally.

'Yes, I will use the same line the next time,' I thought. Just when I had my counter figured, I was never told to shorten my hair again. On any day of the week.

Almost Drowned in the Swimming Pool

May 8, 1976

The two-month long summer holidays started and with it the swimming classes at school. I could not wait to be down to my trunks—called swimming costume by us—in excitement. I ran to jump as far back into the pool as my class one frame would allow. Our coach, Mr R. Sawoo, looked in bewilderment at this flying object, landing with a splash—and then flailing his arms to stay afloat, throat and nose choked with chlorinated water.

Didn't I know how to swim? Of course, I did—I had learnt to over the previous summer holidays. But clearly, I had been a poor student and an overconfident one. Mr Sawoo casually swum to me, picked me up like a sponge and sent me to learn the ABCs of swimming again—hold the perimeter wall, stretch horizontally and get kicking.

I would learn to swim eventually but never the correct way. To this day, I keep my head above water, clearly impeding my movements. And it is the same with all sports for me—high on enthusiasm, poor on technique.

Slapped For Not Becoming a 'Statue'
July 12, 1976

I entered school and someone called out 'statue!' with a finger pointed in my direction. 'What's wrong with him,' I thought and kept walking. He came closer and whacked me; not too hard though. What was that about?

I looked around to see boys standing frozen—like a statue. A game was being played where you were required to go still instantly when someone called 'statue!', staying that way till you heard an 'okay' or 'release'. Failure to comply resulted in a punch or a slap.

Why was everyone afflicted with this madness on a Monday morning, you ask? The movie *Guddi* had been screened the previous evening on television, where Jaya Bhaduri, the female lead, played this game. We were a single channel country, with just a few hours of broadcast daily. The weekly Bollywood film had apparently been seen by almost everyone except me—because it was lights-out for me before the movie screened on television. Leaving me vulnerable to be slapped because I did not know the 'statue!' game.

Most families could not afford television sets at the time, and we ourselves had acquired one recently. Programming was limited, and my parents imposed limits even on the little that was aired. All broadcasts were in black and white till 1982. The brand we owned was Canon—*no relation to the Japanese camera manufacturer*. Most other brands of that era do not exist anymore, including Weston, Beltek, Televista, Crown, Disco, Bigston, Bush, Texla and Uptron.

The Day I Could Have Been Trafficked
August 23, 1976

If I was not busy drowning, I was setting myself to be trafficked. I was surely tripping on something in class one.

The servant—Mohan Singh—used to come to the bus stop on Pandara Road to pick me in the afternoon. On this particular day, he watched the boys alight as usual and the bus leave. I was not amongst them. Panicked, he ran home, alerted my mother, who called my father at his office located on Curzon Road (now called Kasturba Gandhi Marg). There was fear, everyone clueless about what to do other than wait at my bus stop as if I would somehow appear magically.

Voila! I did. After an hour. My parents must have died eight lives by then. A bus coming from the opposite direction stopped and out I came. Holding our school bus driver's hand. Relief and gratitude flowed. Tears too.

Where was I all this while? I had been napping, as I usually did, on the journey back from school and did not wake up on time. When I did, the bus had already reached Greater Kailash. I was a bit disoriented before I realized I had missed getting off at my stop. I approached the driver, a gentle man, who could only ask me to take a seat. He completed his route, reached the depot where all buses are parked, took me to another bus going back in the direction of home and dropped me.

Those were kinder times. I could well have been lost to another world and life had I fallen into the wrong hands.

The Type of Boy Your Parents and Teachers Want You to Be

St. Columba's School's top priority has always been the character development of its students. Get this right and they would be fine men later. The school made its intent known through the spoken and written word at every opportunity to drive home the message. The following extract from the school diary of 1966 outlines these principles clearly:

One who never makes fun of the old or the poor, no matter how decrepit or unfortunate they may be. God's hands rest lovingly on the heads of the aged and the poor.

One who never cheats or is unfair at play. Cheating is contemptible anywhere and at any age. Play should strengthen, not weaken character.

One who never calls bad names, no matter what anybody calls him. You cannot throw mud and keep your own hands clean.

One who is never cruel. Cruelty is the trait of a bully; kindness is the mark of a gentleman.

The boy who never tells lies. Even white lies leave a black spot on the character.

One who never makes fun of a companion because of a misfortune or a handicap which he cannot help.

One who never hesitates to say 'no' when asked to do something which he knows to be wrong.

One who never quarrels. When your tongue gets unruly, lock it in.

One who is always ready to lend a helping hand: at home to his parents, in school to his teacher and his companions.

One who always faces difficulties courageously and cheerfully.

One who does not lament over the evils of the world but tries to make the world better by his example. Remember it is better to light a candle than to curse the darkness.

The Worst Artist Enters a Competition

December 5, 1976

There is only one classification for my drawings: a mess! Only my parents would regard it as art.

Being the apple of their eyes, my parents had heightened expectations of me. I was thus signed up to participate in the annual Shankar's On-the-Spot Painting Competition. It was institutionalised by cartoonist K. Shankar Pillai, the founder of the Children's Book Trust and the International Dolls Museum in Delhi.

I was taken to Bahrisons in Khan Market to stock up on art supplies, and dropped off at Modern School (Barakhamba Road) the following morning. We were required to sit, squat or sprawl on the lawns to draw.

I recall painting a male doctor examining a female patient. At least that's what it looked like to me; the judges must have seen a very different image. I never got to know how I was marked, if anyone even bothered to. Ajay Khanna, who was my latest best friend at the time, received a certificate of merit though—but that's because he truly had talent for art. A handy skill for the architectural career he pursued later in life.

Entered Class Two

January 3, 1977

A new year—I entered class 2-D. Mrs Monica Singh was our designated class teacher. She lived a long life and I reconnected with her at alumni meets four decades later. Time impaired her movements and speech, but she still came out dressed in her bright sarees, hair in a bun, face glowing. Her son, Sanjeet Johar, three years senior to me in school, has become a good friend when we reached our fifties.

Losing My Marbles

1976-78

I always lost my marbles in junior school.

There was a phase when most of us in junior school carried spherical glass marbles in our pockets—to play with whenever there was a window to. Scores of boys could be spotted lost in the game before morning classes started, during the break and for a few stolen minutes between end of school and departure.

The playground was marked with cup sized holes call 'pil'—we twisted the heels of our shoes to make these. The heels would thus wear out at the edges, getting us into trouble at home—shoes would need to be repaired or replaced sooner than expected.

There were various variations of the game, with marbles at stake. I don't recall ever winning. I would always go back home with my pockets lighter. There came a time when I gave up on the gambling, having neither skill nor luck in my favour. I was happy walking around, hands in my pockets, jostling with my marbles. The glass ones.

The Art of Sleeping Through Multiplication Tables
August 8, 1977

I made a habit of falling asleep in the eighth (and last) period of the day. Why? Because each of us had to stand up in turn and recite tables for a number given by Mrs Monica Singh.

It was a calculated move on my part, but luck had to run out some day. I was asked to recite tables for the number three. I did well from three into one equals three till three into eleven equals thirty three. And then I fumbled at the last one, calling three into twelve equals thirty nine. I realized the mistake the instant I said it, but the damage was done. The class spontaneously burst out into laughter, as if to mock me. It was humiliating, for at least a few moments till the next boy was asked to recite tables.

Bullied Into Bringing 'Protection' Money from Home

September 16, 1977

I made a ruckus at home before leaving for school. I wanted Re 1. My father kept refusing but I did not relent in my demand. Eventually he gave in; I know it was not an insignificant sum for him.

What did I need the money for? My safety. A senior boy had walked up to me the previous day, threatening to beat me up if I did not give him a rupee the following day. I was too scared to defy him.

I spotted him from a distance during the break and ran to the classroom to hide. Rahul Rastogi asked what happened and I hushed him into silence, peeping out of the window to track the bully.

I never had to pay up. The bully was probably just messing with me; he looked through me each time our paths crossed. He didn't even seem to remember me or the extortion.

What did I do with the money? Spent on Orange Bars—ice lollies costing 50 paise, or a half a rupee at the time.

When Fifty Paise Bought You a Treat

An Orange Bar—ice lolly—cost 50 paise when we were in junior school. It was a summer treat you had once in a while and a nightmare for mothers because we invariably dripped the orange juice onto our white shirts. Luxury was a Mango

Duet or a Choco Bar costing Rs 2 . A Coca Cola cost Re 1 and 20 paise.

Food prices in the canteen did not rise much when we moved to middle school. A dripping chana kulcha cost 35 paise, while a chola bhatura packed in cheap plastic wrappers quoted 50 paise. Patties were marked 25 paise and a Volga mutton burger 50 paise.

You got hilarity on the side at the south Indian kiosk. A vada, idli or dosa cost an average of 50 paise—these would come floating in sambar in a shallow plastic plate. The boys would slurp the sambar away, calling out 'Anna, more sambar … '

Anna was the vendor distinguishable in a knee-high dhoti wrapped around his waist and a prominent sandalwood ash tikka on his forehead. Boys would satiate their hunger with extra 'free' sambar. Anna could only give so much away—so he would keep diluting the vat with hot water. The later in the break you ordered, the more watery and bland the sambar got.

Despite modest prices, most of us did not have pocket money to buy food in the canteen regularly. We carried lunch in our tiffin boxes—popular fare being Kissan jam sandwiches, potato-filled grilled sandwiches also called patties, chapati with vegetables, and eggs. Somehow Anish Tawakley always had a piece of Indian sweets in his box—their home was gifted these regularly—and I would help myself to it since he did not have much of an appetite for them.

I carried a tiffin daily, but would still have deep fried chola bhatura, a cola and Anish's dessert almost daily during my senior years. I had a conceited opinion of my looks but my photographs of the time project a different image. I was heavier set with no glow on my skin—must have been my diet, something I became conscious of only in my late twenties.

Called a Sissy Despite the Gift of Sweets
November 6, 1977

I cringed. We were sitting at the residence of Mrs Monica Singh, the class teacher. My parents had called upon her to offer sweets for Diwali. 'Why would they do this,' I was wondering.

It was so awkward.

To the teacher's credit, I received no special treatment nor any grace marks. She actually called me a sissy at a subsequent Parent-Teacher Meet. The sweets had no effect in sugar-coating her words.

P.T. Classes

Probably the only ridiculous class we had was P.T. or Physical Training. You could call it Physical Torture even though they were meant for Physical Education.

No one looked forward to the weekly sessions because they contributed little. For one, there was no separate attire—we went out in our leather shoes and uniform. The only exception was when we had swimming classes during summers. We were made to jog around the field, gathering dust and building abdominal pain. Then there were the exercises: stretching arms to the count of one-two-three-four … fourteen-fifteen and change at sixteen to next set. We were not coached for any sport, that was for a select few after regular school hours.

For some reason, the majority of trainers had Sharma as their surname—and they were consistently 'cruel'! Always in a foul mood, their language stung as did their kicks, slaps and thorn-laden branches.

Fortunately, P.T. is now better managed with better facilities and suitable attire. You will no longer find students gathering dust on their woollen trousers, leather shoes, sweaters and blazers.

Coca Cola Banned, 'Government Cola' Introduced
November 13, 1977

No more Coca-Cola in India. The Janata Party was now in power, defeating the Indira Gandhi led Congress party for the first time since Independence. They changed laws for non-Indian business entities and producers of the beverage opted to leave the country than comply with the modified rules of the game.

The Government launched its own cola, Double Seven, produced by state-owned Modern Bakeries. It was commonly called 'Sarkari Cola' or 'Government Cola.' There was nothing lucky for the drink despite the sevens in the name, it would lose its fizz to Thums Up and Campa Cola, both launched by private enterprises around the same time to fill the vacuum left by Coca-Cola.

Thums Up was bought out by Coca-Cola when it re-entered the Indian market in the early 1990s. The Campa brand lost its relevance, with a shot at revival when the business conglomerate Reliance bought the brand in 2023.

Who Wants to Play Chit-Photo?
1977-78

Going by the games we played in junior school; it is a wonder none of us is known to have taken to professional gambling.

One such game was Chit-Photo. There was a craze in town to collect low quality versions of trading cards. Approximately the size of playing cards, they had a single-sided image of a cricketer. While these cards were available all over town, most purchases took place at vendors outside our school gates. Each card cost 5 paise or 10 paise, cheaper if you bought a full sheet and cut them up.

The game? Two would play at a time; one would fly a card in the air, and the other would call chit or photo. If it fell blank side up, it was 'chit', else 'photo.' If you called correctly, you gained a card; if not, you gave one. Cards for exchange were pre-decided as each had a perceived value depending on their availability, star value and pose. Mugshots were cheaper but those depicting players in action—bowling, batting, fielding or keeping wickets—commanded a premium.

There were different versions of the game. You could also fly, say, four cards at a time. If you called 'chit' and three were 'photos', you earned one but lost three. I did better at this game than marbles since you relied more on luck than skill.

These cards were published without any authorisation by the players themselves; no royalties were paid naturally. Sunil Gavaskar, Syed Kirmani, Kapil Dev, Clive Lloyd, Mike Gatting, Dennis Lillee, Zaheer Abbas and hundreds of current and past players had a fandom they may barely be aware of; for a short period in history, till a new fad took over.

Entered Class Three
January 4, 1978

This was likely my last year in the Junior School, giving me a grown-up feeling. I say likely because two sections in class four would continue in the same building while three would move to the Middle School. We did not know which ones. For now, I was in 3-D, with Mrs Nazareth as our class teacher.

Sumeet Mehta Stole the Rubber That Went Over My Pencil
March 6, 1978

Sumeet Mehta had an animal shaped rubber (now called eraser) cap on his pencil. Very cute. Only it was mine.

My aunt had brought fancy rubbers for me from the USA and Sumeet could not take his eyes off the one I was using. It went missing from my pencil box during the break; I looked around to find it mounted on his pencil. When I claimed it to be mine, he asserted ownership by saying that even he could have a similar one. Reputed to be a tough character, I surrendered meekly; the rubber forever his. It would be effective on paper, but not in erasing his sins!

Sumeet always had fancy stationery to show off, most of it picked from his uncle's bookshop in neighbouring CJM. And yet he 'stole' from me.

His mother filled in as a substitute when our regular teachers were on leave. She was again over a few days later and, for some inexplicable reason, took me aside for a private lesson in good conduct. 'I hope you are a better-behaved boy since I was here last, and do not trouble your parents,' she said. I could only nod, with a quizzical expression wondering if she had the wrong boy.

What the hell did mother and son smoke at home?

Selling Out Home-Made Bread Rolls for Charity
October 20, 1978

The school was running a fundraiser. We were asked to get any food items from home to sell and the proceeds would go to charity. I got a dozen bread rolls: boiled potatoes wrapped in moist bread and then deep fried. You could buy one for 25 paise.

I went around hawking them but they refused to get picked for what seemed like a long while; it felt worse because others seemed to be doing brisk business. Just when dejection was getting the better of me, one sold. And then another. Within minutes all were gone. What happened? Maybe the boys were not hungry earlier.

The rolls had their fifteen minutes of fame. It seemed half the junior school was seeking me out, wanting a bite of the tasty snack for themselves. I, too, basked in the attention for as long as I could.

I raised Rs 3 for the cause.

Unmusically Yours

Mrs L. Noronha was so good—if only I was not so hoarse.

I can cause mental trauma to those listening to me sing. And can cause accidents on the dance floor with my two left feet holding up my gyrating, clumsy frame. Places of such entertainment should allow me only with hazard lights mounted. My sister would plead with me to keep to the periphery when everyone was dancing at neighbourhood parties, so embarrassed was she of me!

And so I wonder how the likes of Mrs Noronha handled "blasphemous" singing amongst her students; I suppose by taking such hazards of the job on the chin. She was a goddess to us seven-year-olds when her fingers moved on the piano, listening to her sing along as only a music star can. I so wanted to be one half of a duet with her but she might have gone tone deaf had any such act of bravado been attempted. She limited my participation to a jarring note in a group of fifty.

Stretched Cursive to Fill Out Pages Unnecessarily
November 20, 1978

Rahul Rastogi's cursive handwriting was very attractive. He would give it that little extra gap between characters and words, occupying perhaps 20 per cent more space on the page—making it eminently more readable than the insect crawl some of our handwriting resembled. Being a good student, his books had minimal red ink to mar the pages.

I had only a few pages of my class notebook left and I wanted to fill it out so I could ask for a new one within the same academic year. So, I decided to imitate Rahul's style for the writing to take up more space—but I exaggerated a bit too much. I was stretching so much that only two or three words were fitting in one line. My handwriting slid from bad to ridiculous. A summons was sent home, an eraser was provided and I was told to remove and rewrite everything.

Fifth in Class: Did the Gift of an Imported Watch Earn Me Grace Marks?
December 22, 1978

I finished fifth in class—my highest ever rank. I would usually be the seventh or the eighth. What changed?

My parents had been travelling to Germany and the USA, their first overseas trip, for two months leading up to the final exams. I was left under the care of my grandmother, uncle and aunt. The uncle took his role as foster parent a bit too seriously, coming across as a tough taskmaster with my academics. Being a super-achiever himself, a doctor from the top medical institution in the country, must have made him expect heightened levels of diligence from those around him. He even slapped me once for refusing to study; I don't recall ever being hit at home for offences of academic nature. We joke about the slap even to date at family gatherings.

Did this approach make a better scholar of me? My uncle took credit for it, but so did my mother—for putting in all the effort with my homework through the year. Hello, will someone give credit to the student who actually put in the hard work?

Mrs Nazareth had hinted at, and my parents had obliged, getting a watch from the USA. I am sure it did not influence the grades.

The Five Who Would Cry for Not Finishing First in Class

Venkatram Krishnaswamy, Vikramjit Mukherjee, Saeed-ul-Islam, Dinesh Sehgal and Rahul Rastogi seemed to have cornered the market for the top five positions in class. The one who finished first was always beaming on the day report cards were handed out. The other four looked devastated—and at least one or two of them would be in tears, literally, with their parents looking no less glum. How did they cope with such pressure? We were infants!

Ajay Khanna and I, best friends for a while, would finish a notch or two below them. But we both broke their 'cartel' in Middle School by rising up the ranks, causing further misery to the five. No one understood why they would get so emotional!

The Latest Commodity on the Trading Floor: Airline Labels

There was a new commodity in school: airline baggage stickers, the ones you write your name and address on for identification. A relic now.

Your status was determined by your collection, measured by the quantity you owned and how rare those were. There was a scramble to get our hands on any we could. Easiest source were friends and family taking a flight—not common in those times though. We would request them to pick extra stickers for us while checking in. The most were those of domestic carrier Indian Airlines, unsurprising as it was a state run monopoly at the time. Air India, the national carrier across borders, was not uncommon either. Then came other international airlines. Vendors sitting outside school gates got onto the game—selling these stickers. God only knew who fed this supply chain!

We built our collection by trading these stickers. The value was determined by both parties on the spot. My father had to go the airport occasionally to pick and drop his seniors in Government; his access enabled him to pick a few stickers for me. I became rich in capital (of airline stickers) but poor trading skills diluted my holdings. When negotiating an exchange, I would always be egged on by onlookers to accept the offer from the other party—only to be laughed at after the deal was done. It seemed everyone was out to sabotage my interests.

The fad lasted a few months, before all of us boarded a flight to seek another muse.

Entered Class Four: The Year Would Be Fifteen Months Long
January 8, 1979

Class four came with surprises.

I was moved to 4-A, away from section D. Many of us were shuffled this way, all but a handful restored to their original sections when they entered class five. I did not get the logic of this, but it enabled me to bond with students from Section A too. We got a brilliant class teacher, Mrs J. Wintle.

We were also kept back in the Junior School. There were temporary structures outside of the main building; classes 4-A and 4-B were accommodated there. For the supposedly flimsy material used, these rooms have been standing firm for over fifty years. I would have to wait another year before being promoted to Middle School.

The school decided to shift the academic year. Instead of running from January to December, it would henceforth be from April to March, a norm in other schools already. Class four would start in January as usual, but end in March the following year making it fifteen months long.

Interestingly, my cousin studying in Ambala in Convent of Jesus and Mary School, a co-ed, had to go through the same change. But their school accommodated two academic years in fifteen months. We were in the same grade earlier, but he became senior to me by one year as a consequence.

Br Morrissey Passes Away; We Get Two Holidays

While in class four, we were met with sombre news in the morning: the Middle School headmaster Br J.U. Morrissey had passed away and school would be closed for two days. We were instructed to return home.

Our first reaction? Br. Morrissey was very strict and we will not have to interact with him when we move to the Middle School the following year. And we viewed the two days off as play time.

There were many instances when school had to be shut unexpectedly and always was for unfortunate reasons. Rather than evoke empathy amongst us boys, we would seek delight in the time off from school rather commiserate with the cause of the closure.

Deaths and injuries were reported due to unrest at the adjoining Bangla Sahib Gurudwara—an important place of worship for Sikhs and other Punjabis—leading to imposition of curfew; we were closed for three days when I was in class three. Invariably, the Middle School basement would get flooded on severe monsoon days forcing suspension of classes; Delhi does not get such intense rain anymore due to climate change. The longest break came during the riots following the assassination of Indira Gandhi. These are just some instances; when we should have been concerned about the reasons for the school to be closed, we just went out and had a good time!

Slapped for Shooting With 'Gun' on Holi
March 12, 1979

'Isn't he the man who slapped me on the street for spraying Holi water on him? Yes, he was. What's he doing in the school?'

We had gone to visit family friends in Pandara Road the previous day and had been playing with water pistols outside their house in excitement of Holi, the festival of colours, just a few days away. We were pointing our guns at passers-by and they would playfully trot away. Until a 'humourless' man got 'shot.' I kept firing, ignoring his calls to stop. The book he was using as a shield and his shirt got wet.

When I did not relent, he came up to me and gave me the hardest whack I have received in my life. I just about managed to balance myself from toppling into a deep drain running along the road. I would have been severely injured had I fallen in. The man walked away, my friends not sure whether to console me or burst out laughing.

Lo and behold! The next day I saw the same man in school. He looked through me as if he had never seen me before. Maybe there are too many little boys he punishes on streets to be able to keep track of. I, later, learnt he was Mr Reginald Rocha, a teacher in the school, not to be confused with his gentler sibling, Mr Peter Rocha who would be my class teacher in eleventh and twelfth.

A Rubber Lizard Results in High Fever

April 13, 1979

I bought a rubber toy lizard to spook my mother. I developed a fever instead.

A vendor outside the school gate sold cheap rubber toys—animals and birds. I bought a few, including a lizard, because I knew the presence of a real one creeps my mother out. It still does and my sister has taken after her. I derived perverse joy in their screams when I planted the fake lizard on them later in the afternoon.

I looked forward to a highly satisfying sleep that night but came down with a fever instead. There were no textbook explanations, and the doctor could not figure a suitable prescription. Come morning, my mother spotted the 'lizard' and threw it out in disgust. By afternoon, my fever was back to normal, and I was playing badminton in the evening. Had the lizard cast a spell? I would have been dismissed as superstitious hogwash if I had not fallen sick in a similar fashion twice in as many years—each time I brought a toy lizard home.

Go figure!

A Typical Day Was Like …

A school day had a fixed pattern for me and there was no deviating from it. If teachers kept us line in school, my mother maintained it at home.

Wake up in the morning, get dressed, have breakfast, complete any homework if pending, catch the school bus in the morning and back in the afternoon. Lunch was followed by an hour long siesta. Homework time after that—my mother would assist up to class three; I had to do it myself after that. We had to finish most of it in the afternoon itself before being allowed to go out and play.

I spent about two hours out every evening, playing badminton or cricket mostly. Or cycling. Come back home to finish any pending homework and prepare for any upcoming tests. I was allowed to watch a bit of television if time permitted. Dinner would be around eight and lights out at ten. To wake to another typical day the following morning, unless it was a holiday.

Screening a 'Soft Porn' Film for Junior School Boys
July 13, 1979

Without any prior intimation, we were called out of our class for a screening of the Bollywood film *Heera Panna*. No idea why we got this double treat. One, we were taken out for a movie during class hours. And two, for its explicit scenes, bold by the standards of the 1970s. And certainly not suitable for those barely ten years old.

Starring Dev Anand, Zeenat Aman and Rakhee Gulzar, you had women in bikinis and the protagonists engaging in pre-marital relationships. Our quarter-adult minds relished the scenes without necessarily understanding what was happening. I watched it again later in my adulthood out of curiosity; one will need special talents to produce a film worse than this.

What came over the Brothers to screen a movie like this for us?

The Murders of Sanjay and Geeta Chopra Rock the Nation. And Shake Our Parents.
August 29, 1979

Everyone was talking about the murders of Sanjay and Geeta Chopra, siblings aged fourteen and sixteen respectively. Their bodies were discovered by a cowherd on the Delhi Ridge the previous evening.

Children of Madan Mohan Chopra, a captain in the Indian Navy, they took a lift from strangers on their way to All India Radio for the recording of a youth program, *Yuva Vani*. They were kidnapped instead, the culprits hoping to demand a ransom since the two children looked like they were from a rich family. When the kidnappers realized their father was just an armed forces officer of modest means, they were harassed and murdered.

The case captured the imagination of the nation, with Prime Minister Morarji Desai demanding a thorough and speedy investigation. The culprits were captured within a fortnight; their names Billa and Ranga forever becoming synonymous with villains. They were convicted and were eventually hanged on January 31, 1982.

As is usually the case in these matters, conspiracy theories floated. About powerful politicians being behind the rape and murder, Billa and Ranga being no more than fall guys. Confessions were extracted by inducing drugs in them. An alternate truth, if any, would never be known.

Although we were too young to leave home on our own, we were warned against ever taking a lift from strangers. The message was drilled into us repeatedly for years to come.

Collective Shame: We Want a Holiday Because Jayaprakash Narayan Died.
October 8, 1979

The middle school had assembled on the grounds as usual after the break when Br Eric D'Souza announced the demise of Jayaprakash Narayan, a highly respected political activist and one of the key leaders responsible for Indira Gandhi's loss in the last general elections.

While the headmaster conveyed the news in a grave tone, all the boys spontaneously broke out into a chant: 'We want a holiday, we want a holiday … '

The headmaster gave it back to us for only thinking of a holiday, showing scant respect where it was due. He chided us for our thinking, for our values. I am sure he was tempted to let Charlie have a word with each of us personally.

We did not get a day off even as national flags were flown at half mast during the official period of mourning across the country.

How Could a Teacher Rape a Student?
October 24, 1979

'How many of you know of or have a lawyer or judge in the family?'

Mrs Jyoti Kumar had a worried look on her face when she asked the question. A few boys volunteered names. I had one to offer too—but wasn't sure how to articulate it. A close uncle was a judge in the Tis Hazari courts—but I did not know how to mention the name of the court in English. Was it Thirty Thousand? No, it did not make sense. Tis Hazar is thirty thousand in Hindi. Eventually I went up and shared my uncle's name, muttering Tis Hazari with embarrassment. I was not aware that there was only one name for it.

Why did she need these names? There were stories doing the rounds of her husband having been arrested—for either raping or sleeping with a girl under eighteen. She used to come to his residence for tuitions where the incident took place. Who was the girl? Some said she was from CJM and daughter of one of our faculty. We never learnt the complete truth.

Mrs Kumar was never seen after the day she took the names from us. Her husband was sentenced to seven years in prison for statutory rape according to a newspaper article.

Charity Begins at Home
November 22, 1979

'If you think you are a loser, you are never going to win.'

That's the moral delivered to the audience of *SMIKE*, a grand pop musical put together by our school, marking the 'International Year of the Child.' A tribute to children all over the world, *SMIKE* by Roger Holman and Simon May was based on the early chapters of Charles Dickens' *Nicholas Nickleby*. The play is named after Smike, an orphaned waif at Dotheboys Hall, the boarding school of the infamous villain, Mr. Squeers.

The production was initiated by Br Morrissey, who passed away before the curtains went up. Br Eric D'Souza took the direction and choreography upon himself, ably supported by the love of every Columban, Mrs R. Sudon. Reviewers gave five stars to the sets and costumes depicting boarding houses and characters of nineteenth century England, as also to the music of Rocky Fernandes. The five shows were sold out, meeting its goals of raising Rs 2,50,000 to purchase computers while drawing attention to the plight of underprivileged children in India.

I enjoyed the play but I did not comprehend the story at all. I would recall a big sign reading 'Charity Begins at Home', wondering for years what it meant.

Being a fundraiser, our parents were asked to make a donation. My father sent Rs 21; Br D'Souza returned it, expecting a more generous contribution. It was raised to Rs 51. It was accepted with a further look of disappointment.

Moral Science Was a Subject

Right through school, we had a weekly period called Moral Science. To inculcate in us the right values, not just in theory but in action too.

The classes were a mixed bag. We had workbooks with exercises—since everything was subjective, there would be animated discussions on how situations illustrated in the books should have been handled, what decisions should have been taken. The engagement also varied with the teacher—some were very interested, some not so.

The likes of Mr Pokhriyal observed life keenly and liked to share lessons he himself learnt. Like narrating the sight of a homeless man who found a stale chapati in a garbage bin, only to be challenged for it by a street dog. He witnessed the struggle of two hungry souls from the school bus Z16 and promised to never waste a morsel of food in his plate and would urge every student to never waste anything.

As much as possible, we tried to eke out a free period for ourselves. To chat away or finish our class work. It suited supervising teachers who used the opportunity to mark any pending papers or take care of administrative work.

The Poor Fund Box was a permanent feature though. It would be passed around regularly to drop any loose change we could spare. Moments like those were times to make a decision: should the twenty five paise go to the needy or to the vendor selling patties in the break? Did it hone our ability to take life decisions in the future?

You Do Not Win a Lady's Affections by Throwing Yourself on Her
November 29, 1979

If you think only boys lusted after teachers, some of the male tutors did not conduct themselves any more honourably.

Everyone had the hots for Ms A. Cooke but you could not make your desire known. Mr J. Mascarenhas believed he was being discreet but anyone travelling in his bus would have seen through his intent. He insisted on sitting next to Ms Cooke in the double seat daily—so he could lean onto her "accidentally" whenever the bus negotiated roundabouts or sharp turns.

The teacher might have noticed the indiscretion but may have chosen silence to maintain her dignity. She did not stay in the school for long. Would she have moved anyway or did a male staffer drive her away?

Too Bright for His Class, Solves Senior Exam with Ease
December 12, 1979

Rahul Rastogi solved a senior's mathematics paper. Show off! Cheating in exams was controlled by mixing grades. One row would be of class four students, the next of class five and further alternating like this. Rohit Srivastava's stress during exams was a spectacle in itself—especially when it came to mathematics. His struggles seemed more difficult to manage when he spotted Rahul Rastogi writing away effortlessly. With half an hour left, Rahul stopped, a perplexed look on his face. 'Ha, he's not so smart,' Rohit thought comforting himself. The invigilator was called, there was a discussion and then a bomb went off: Rahul had been solving the senior grade paper, which had been handed over to him by mistake!

Rohit was enraged at the injustice of it all. He could barely solve his own grade's paper, and the bugger was already a year ahead in his smarts! Why the inequality in distribution of brain power?

Of course, Rahul had to start all over again with the correct paper; he finished second in the class that year.

'Drugged' Churan and Chilli Chips at School Gates

I wonder who allowed vendors to sell the kind of food items they did outside the school gates?

They carried saucy tamarind sticks, spiced kamrak (star fruit), groundnuts in season and chips—plain and chilli. The last mentioned were wafers, really, in small plastic packets, and I would sometimes take the hotter variety for my mother. She enjoyed having something spicy with Coca Cola, a late morning ritual she maintained for over seventy years of life before diabetes denied her the daily 'high.' Groundnuts were our favourite winter snack, although despised by the bus driver and conductor. We littered the floor with shells within minutes—a nightmare to clean later.

And then there was churan—a digestive powder packaged in a straw-like sealed tube. You stayed away from those who had it lest you get caught in the resulting 'aromatic' waft of air emanating from their mouth or backside. Some who consumed claimed a heady feeling, lending credence to rumours of the churan being laced with drugs to improve their saleability. Some mothers warned their sons against having it but only an exception heeded the advice.

The Day I Peed in My Trousers in Class
January 11, 1980

You could not go to the bathroom without permission which was hard to come by while the class was on. The best time was between classes if you could pull off a rush job. Teachers came in and left with clockwork precision, with the window barely longer than a minute or two when one teacher packed up and the next settled in.

The English literature class was on, I was desperate to go, the cold made it worse. Mrs Wintle was in a stern mood, the expression warning anyone dare 'piss' her with an interruption. Pee in your pants, but do not disturb the flow of the lecture was the unspoken message to us (Puns galore!). I obeyed.

Yes, I was left with no choice but to pee in my woollen trousers. When the pressure got unbearable, I thought releasing a drop or two would ease it. The drop became a trickle, before everything in the bladder came gushing out. Liquid spilling on the floor through my trousers was making a sound and I prayed Pavan Vaish, sitting in front of me, does not get alerted.

I went about the rest of the day hoping no one would notice my wet trousers. I reached home, told no one and wore the trousers as it is the rest of the season. No one smelt a rat or the pee. The trousers would eventually be sent for annual dry-cleaning when we switched to white cotton trousers of the summer uniform.

Class Photo: A Special Day

Attendance would be highest the day our class photos were taken. Our uniforms would be perfectly ironed and clean and all, but the grumpy ones would be at their smiling or grinning best. No one wanted to be missing out in *The Columban*, our annual school magazine. We had the option to buy a copy of the class photograph; I usually did.

The distribution of the magazine was another day to look forward to. Read up on news of the year gone by and see us and others featured in it. Siblings received only one copy between them; yes, the school was thorough in maintaining these lists. Printing of the magazine took place at Gondal's Press, run by an ex-Columban, for many years. He charged thirty-five rupees per copy, unchanged for a long time, paid to the school by us.

Entered Class Five: No More Pencils, Fountain Pens for Us

April 1, 1980

Class five is a watershed year—that's when we get promoted from using pencils to pens. Fountain pens to be specific—ball points or any other pens were against the rules. Suddenly one felt grown up, even though it was a nightmare for mothers who had to clean stained uniforms.

Ink pots had to be carried daily or locked in our desks. Ink on our clothes would be a regular feature—spilled or broken bottles, leaked pens or boys just spraying on each other. Even bags and books were not spared stains, big and small.

Ink could also wake Charlie from a peaceful nap—Mukul and Nelson once got into an ink fight but Yogesh Sehgal got reprimanded by Charlie too—Yogesh was sitting behind them, guffawing. Any of us could have been collateral damage for being at the scene of crime, enjoying the entertainment.

I was moved back into section D with Mrs U. Das as our class teacher. More significantly, we were in the world dominated by the headmaster of the Middle School, Br Eric Steve D'Souza. Everyone admired him, everyone feared him. But everyone yearned to be his student.

Brother Eric Steve D'Souza Could Have Been Anyone

He could have been Bill Gates or Steve Jobs—he had what they had, probably more. Coincidentally, all born in the

1950s. But Br Eric Steve D'Souza did not use his brain to make billions; rather, he crossed wires with his heart so his soul could resonate with the likes of Mahatma Gandhi, Nelson Mandela and Martin Luther King. People who could have been anyone but choosing to serve those who needed them the most.

Mr Pokhriyal, the singing Mathematics teacher in senior school, had an apt song for Br D'Souza:

Apne liye, jiye to kya jiye (If you lived for yourself then what is that living)

To jee, ay dil, zamaane ke liye (So live, my heart, for this world)

Br D'Souza was a brilliant academician. Not just in what he was formally trained for, but also with an uncanny ability to grasp new subjects like computer programming. He could easily be a student and his own tutor.

He was a musician, a theatre director, a quizmaster and a sportsman who could dribble a football, swing a cricket ball and wield a hockey stick. His had a mind whirring all the time, with a photographic memory, able to pull out any information quicker than a computer. He and Charlie could give you sore bottoms and yet be your friend, your confidant, your mentor. He never forgot anyone, nor their strengths and weaknesses—he would be there to bolster the former and aid with the latter. Because above everything else, he was a teacher in every sense of the word.

He could have stayed on in St. Columba's School, in the centre of the country, and soaked in all the adulation. But he moved away—to obscure Shillong before hitting thirty-five.

His best years were yet to come and he felt an impoverished region needed him more than a glitzy city. He would go on to don the hat of a social entrepreneur, setting up the Providence School from scratch. For those who were too poor to even afford free Government education—to train them in skills so they could earn a livelihood and lead a life of dignity and hope.

Br D'Souza travelled a long way in a short while: from the rebellious spirit of the 1960s with his long hair, John Lennon glasses and infectious charisma to the educationist, the missionary at ease in a modest cassock. Son of an army officer, he joined the Christian Brotherhood at sixteen. He touched thousands directly and many more through them, but his sensitivity, his empathy made everyone feel he was there only for them, so deep was his connection to each. His life was defined by his deep and unwavering commitment to his students, his belief in the power of education to transform lives—it was the source of his youthfulness, his energy, his faith.

The conviction of his calling and his honesty allowed him to speak his mind. He forged his own, always thinking ahead and always seeking new ways to inspire, educate and uplift.

Those who knew him admired him but feared his chain smoking would cut short his stay, like many geniuses who did not live long. Instead, Progressive Supranuclear Palsy (PSP) got to him first, a cruel fate for someone who donated all of God's gifts to improve lives other than his own.

Whether he taught you directly or not, every Columban who was there during Br D'Souza's time feels blessed to have walked the same corridors as he did. He left an indelible mark on each of us and there would be no better tribute than to imbibe and practice all the values he himself led with. He was the alchemist whose students turned 24K gold.

If you were seeking him, he would be found amid his students. Even now, we just have to look around and he will be there—smiling, laughing, singing, joking. To bond and to disarm you. So he could ram into us a sense of discipline, an understanding of what it takes to be an upright human being. Ensuring we apply ourselves to what we decide to do, bringing out the best versions of ourselves.

And yet, even he would need some assistance at times so his boys, his children, could be what they were meant to be. That's why Br D'Souza's God sent a sidekick along, responding to the name, Charlie.

The Many Names of Br D'Souza

Brother Eric Steve D'Souza
Dasu
Brother Steve
Steve
Eric
Kavua (Crow)
Chooza
ESD
Every Superman's Dream

We Could Have Been Sanskrit Scholars or Theatre Artists!

April 30, 1980

Had Mr Brij Mohan Shah continued teaching us, some of us could have become Sanskrit scholars or theatre personalities. Unfortunately, he left within a month of being assigned to teach us Sanskrit in class five.

He was a mesmerising force in the classroom, making us love the subject. We wondered why he was so animated as a teacher, until we learnt he was an alumnus of the National School of Drama. At some stage, he must have figured teaching Sanskrit to middle school boys will not make this world a happier place but bringing stories to life would. He returned to his alma mater as a teacher, eventually running the show as its director. He would go on to act in and direct many popular plays and films.

His replacement Mrs Handa, competent no doubt, would address the room as if at a funeral service; the school should have provided smelling salts had any of us passed out expecting dead men to walk in with her.

Carpool

For about two years, we went to school in a carpool.

We lived in Kaka Nagar in central Delhi for a while, not too far from school. The colony, as neighbourhoods are referred to, had many studying in St. Columba's and CJM.

Mr Wadhwa, our next door neighbour, suggested we form a car pool and we agreed.

By turn, a parent would pick and drop kids daily. We had an Ambassador, the others had the more compact Premier Padmini or commonly called Fiat. There were seven children, ranging from class two to six: Sanjay and Seema Wadhwa, Siddhartha and Rohini Dhingra, Pia Banerjee, my sister Smita and me. And the parent driver. Mrs Dhingra was a teacher in CJM and would anyway take her car daily to school. When it was her turn, she just had to pack in her two children and the rest of us.

At some point, the car pool was discontinued. Don't know who initiated it. And we were back to school buses. Certainly more fun than going with the same boring crowd daily.

Cub for a Year, Never a Scout
May 12, 1980

I went on my first school trip—a scout camp in Kausani in the Himalayas. Boy, was it a stinky one!

I had joined as a cub in class five and it required me to stay back every Friday. My father would send his junior, Mr Ajesh, to pick me from school and drop me home on his Rajdoot motorcycle. I don't recall ever exchanging a word with him, not even a thank you. It would only be many years later when I got comfortable exchanging niceties with people.

The trip was quite an exposure for me. Camping in tents and bunk beds was a first. Toilet was a hole in the ground in an enclosure of canvas; you had to hang your hat on a supporting bamboo pole to mark it your private territory temporarily. After the job was done, you covered the dump with mud excavated when the hole was dug. You took a mug of water with you to clean up; toilet paper was a rarity at that time. I do not recall how we washed hands after we came out. Bathing and laundry was not an option. We could have been mistaken for skunks before the trip was over. If nature called at night, we were advised to go into the forested area surrounding the camp site, keeping an eye out for leopards. There was no directive on what to do had we come face to face with one.

We sat around a bonfire daily when it got dark. That's where we had dinner, cracked jokes, shared stories, sung and even put up staged performances. Salil Kapoor went an extra mile to put a skit together but was denied permission last minute despite him being the seniormost scout. Why? One of the faculty was travelling with his daughter who had been cast in the play. But girls were not allowed at a scout campfire and no exception would be made. Salil called off the show and sulked the rest of the trip. He was not seen at subsequent bonfires.

Mr C. Innis, who would be my class teacher in eighth, managed the scout movement in Columba's. I had to memorise a pledge and recite it at the camp to be officially inducted and receive my badge. I stressed preparing for it but realized I would have been taken in even if I had fluffed my lines.

We were taken on a half day trip to the popular hill station, Nainital. I had been given Rs 30 to spend; I used it to purchase gifts for my parents and a paper mache tribal face mask from a handicrafts shop. The latter would hang at the entrance of our home for two years to ward off the evil eye.

I would have been eligible to be a scout the following year but dropped out. Maybe the toilet and lack of a bath for a week was too much of a hygiene trauma for me.

When Martyr Badluram Saved His Regiment From Starvation
May 17, 1980

The return journey from the scout camp was no less entertaining than the trip itself. With two distinct memories standing out.

The bus was running late due to traffic jams—we stopped at a dhaba, a roadside eatery, where I ordered a deep-fried aloo parantha to have in the bus. When I think back about it, I still regret not having packed two—it was absolutely yummy and one was not enough to satiate my appetite.

The other was the song we sang over and over again, the lyrics go as:

> *Ek khubsurat ladki thi …*
> *Usko dekh ke rifleman …*
> *Chindi khichna bhul gaya …*
> *Havaldar Major dekh liya …*

Usko pittu lagaya ...
Badluram ek sipahi thaa ...
Japan war me mar gaya ...
Quarter Master smart thaa ...
Usney ration nikala ...
Badluram ka badan zamin ke nichey hain ...
Toh humein uska ration milta hain ...
Sabashh ... hallelujah ...
Toh humein uska ration milta hain ...

It narrates the legend of a soldier, Badluram, who is killed by the Japanese in the Second World War. The Quarter Master did not report it and continued drawing rations in his name. The surplus thus enabled the regiment to survive when surrounded by enemies, their supplies cut off. So the song goes on to how Badluram is buried but other soldiers still get rations in his name. Major M.T Proktar wrote this song in memory of the soldier and set the tune to Pete Seeger's song, *John Brown's Body*. It is now an established tradition for the Assam Regiment to recite this song at their passing out parade.

Face-to-Face With Charlie

Every Columban has met Charlie. You could be a role model of a student, exemplary in your behaviour, well turned out, courteous, boasting grades to make any parent proud and yet, at least once if not more, Charlie would have beckoned you.

You would have to respond with an outstretched arm or by bending over.

So who is Charlie? There is no simple answer. Or a singular one. Charlie was our guardian angel. Watching over us, shaping the best version of us. Brothers and other teachers have come and gone, but Charlie had a burden to bear and thus could not be anywhere but within the school premises. A permanent fixture, resident and member of the staff. Never featured in faculty photographs and yet a more dominant presence than any to have walked the corridors of St. Columba's.

That is why we are Charlie's Boys. The chosen ones. We would wish Charlie away every single day of our time in school and yet express gratitude where it is due. But for Charlie, we may not have become who we are.

Charlie watched over us every single minute of every single day while we were in school. Out of concern, out of care. To keep us in line. So we may excel. Not so much in quantifiable parameters like grades and medals but in our attitude and approach. Applying ourselves, being diligent, delivering on time was more important than the outcome. We may be boys but our conduct had to be of gentlemen. We did not need to be stylish or sport fine attire but our thoughts had to be lofty. No matter the room we walked into in life, heads should turn because others would know they are in the company of one of Charlie's Boys.

No mean task.

Three thousand of us at any given time, generations passing through the gates over decades. How can anyone manage this without spirits flagging, energies sapping? Not very difficult if you have the magic potion where you derive your power from. Charlie had it. It can be defined and described in one word.

Fear.

Yes, you can invoke oodles of it when you are a cane. Yes, that's what Charlie was. A cane. A metaphor too. For any object that could be picked to inflict bodily hurt. When there was none handy, there were always the hands and the legs to beat the hell out of us.

Not that Charie needed to be in physical contact with us each time to be effective. Because it was a force higher than that. It's mere existence was deterrent enough, was enough to make hardy workers of us, was enough to incite fear for us to be at our best behaviour.

Of course, the relationship between Charlie and us was one of respect and tolerance. We learnt to bear the pain, maintaining a dignified silence about our interactions but it did not mean we tempted Charlie. That's where fear worked: not only did we not want to be hit, we did not want to invite a teacher's ire and be in their bad books. A glare, a reprimand, a scolding or any other form of public humiliation was no less a deterrent than a physical whack.

We could never let our guard down. Charlie was always on the prowl. Seeking the next culprit. Or victim. Who you were depended on which side of the divide you were on.

Yet there was never any loathing or hate for Charlie. We were a family, taking everyone and everything in our stride. For no matter where we are in life, we will always have a dual identity, like two sides of a coin. No one can take that away from us.

We are Columbans.

And we are Charlie's Boys.

The Many Avatars of Charlie

Of course, Charlie had to have a tangible form to be effective. For there is truth in 'spare the rod, spoil the child' if applied with moderation and mindfully. As the ones at the receiving end, we saw Charlie coming at us in various avatars:

Charlie 1: This was the thin cane. Caused shooting pain upon contact but recovery was relatively quicker.

Charlie 2: The thick cane. Did not hurt as much initially but the pain lingered longer. Preferred weapon in winters since we were padded up with warm clothes and the thin one would not sting.

When any of the Brothers were in a kind mood, they allowed us to choose from the Charlies. If not or if there was no time to be wasted, they just grabbed whatever was handy and whacked us! On the palm or on the backside—we were required to bend over, resting our hands on our knees or against a wall or a desk. We could not see Charlie in this posture, but could hear the swoosh as it came down in an arc.

The ruler: Its edge struck on your knuckles or its flat surface on your palm. The movement was gentle, the impact was not.

The leg of a chair: Became infamous in the hands of Mr Ram, the crafts teacher. This was the version we were genuinely scared of.

Thorn-laden branches: In the sports field by Mr 'Bloodif' Sharma. He plucked one from any nearby tree when required, disposed of after use (or abuse).

The hand: To slap anywhere—face, head, neck, back and shoulders.

Foot, attached to a leg: To kick anywhere, its reach determined by the agility of the limb.

Feather duster stripped bare: Used for cleaning desks, they would eventually lose their feathers leaving a juicy stick to beat with. A fashion statement too, since a few colourful feathers would still be sticking to it. An odd one would transfer and stick to our clothes, branding us as the irksome one.

The blackboard duster: When teachers lost their patience and acted before they thought of the consequences. We would pray they are good at the sport; the velocity, angle and direction had to be perfect to strike the offender. It was thus critical for each of us to be alert lest we get struck. In most cases though, some other poor fellow would bear the brunt. Of course, no apology or remorse would be forthcoming in such cases.

Summer Holidays: Time to Get Bored

Summer holidays were almost two months long, starting early May. We could not wait for days of no classes, only to pass the time doing absolutely nothing.

Vacations? All of us did not go. If we did, it was to grandparents, uncles and aunts living in other towns. Most of ours lived in Delhi itself. Being in the Government, my father was entitled to one paid family holiday annually under the LTC (Leave Travel Concession) scheme; we travelled by train and stayed in Government guest houses called Circuit House or Inspection Bungalow for about a week.

The rest of the days were spent at home. We read a lot of books, even when roasting in the heat. Electric supply was erratic, desert coolers worked up to a point and air-conditioning was unaffordable until much later in life. Evenings were spent playing badminton or football in the neighbourhood. Holiday homework was handed out to keep us productive but it was usually a rush job closer to the end of the break.

But boredom allowed us to dream—at night and in the day. Conjuring up futures and figuring what it would take to create those. We would return to school, batteries re-charged. Raring to go—not at our books but everything games and mischief.

Sanjay Gandhi Killed in Plane Crash, Nation Embarks on Different Flight Path

June 23, 1980

My parents and I were consulting Dr Neera Bajaj at the Government run CGHS Dispensary located within the Constitution Club of India premises on Rafi Marg when the news came in. Sanjay Gandhi, the powerful and not necessarily popular son of Prime Minister Indira Gandhi, died when he was trying an acrobatic manoeuvre in a two-seater plane after taking off from Safdarjung Airport. He was thirty three. And an alumnus of St. Columba's High School. He was tipped to occupy the 'throne' of power after his mother.

His death left the nation stunned; conspiracy theories followed, including outlandish ones pointing to Indira Gandhi plotting her son's death. Sanjay Gandhi had gained infamy for assuming extra-constitutional powers, his excesses 'pardoned' by the high offices occupied by his family. His failed attempt to make a people's car under the brand Maruti, and forced sterilisation of millions of poor men during the Emergency to check population growth, were just two examples flagged by (what was then a relatively freer) media but there was no authority to check him.

His funeral procession was a show of power in itself despite the mother and his brother, Rajiv Gandhi, clearly stricken by grief. Four hundred thousand people were estimated to have lined up the streets to watch his final journey. It went down Rajpath, crossing India Gate, to the cremation site at Shanti Van—only luminaries like his grandfather, Jawaharlal Nehru, had been accorded such an honour. Him being taken down the same path came as no surprise despite never holding any administrative positions officially. We were living in Kaka Nagar, walking distance from India Gate, and were part of this crowd too.

I was in Class five and could barely grasp what this event meant for the country. All sorts of analyses and predictions followed but no pundit was able to grasp what was to follow. Rajiv Gandhi, the reluctant politician, would be thrust into family matters. In just over a decade, Indira Gandhi and Rajiv Gandhi too would be met with violent deaths. India would change significantly during the current and subsequent decades to follow—its values, economy, social fabric, politics and its relationship with religion. There is one question people still ask but can never come up with a plausible answer: What if Sanjay Gandhi had lived?

Charlie Does Not Approve Smoking Your Pencil
July 18, 1980

Lightning does not strike the same spot twice but Charlie could. Rohit Valia's bottoms learnt it the hard way, literally. Br D'Souza made a surprise entrance into the classroom, pulled Rohit out, made him bend over, swinging Charlie to land twice at exactly the same spot. His crime? Smoking on the back benches. Not a cigarette, but his pencil. There was no smoke, but the headmaster saw fire. We fancied ourselves as grown-ups by now, so why expect to be punished with kid gloves?

Rohit learnt his lesson well. He does not smoke even now.

The Singing Maths Teacher Shares Business Management Lesson

July 28, 1980

'I will give a Cadbury's chocolate éclair to anyone who can solve the sum on the blackboard,' challenged Mr Pokhriyal.

'I will give two if you can solve it,' called out a backbencher.

The new mathematics teacher was not going to have it easy. He was assigned 12-A, boasting amongst the brightest set of minds to come together in a classroom. They were preparing to get through to the prestigious IITs and AIIMS, but Mr Pokhriyal was trained to teach the milder ISCE board curriculum. Students realized this and would hurl challenges he was not equipped to solve, stressing him out.

He was a true teacher—he did not lower the bar to bring students to his level but raised it for himself. He devised a win-win: the class would take up IIT level challenges and students and teacher would try to solve them at the same time. Inadvertently, he had stumbled upon a lesson for future CEOs: leaders cannot always be expected to offer ideas and solutions, so it is best to bring others into giving it a shot. He adopted it as one of his teaching mantras over a long career. The master did not always win, taking pride in the brilliance of his students.

Sitting in the class was Sanjeev Bikhchandani who would go on to become a poster boy of tech entrepreneurship, founding and investing in many a venture including *Naukri.com*, India's biggest job portal. Seems he paid attention to more than the equations on the blackboard.

Mr Pokhriyal became the talk of the school very early on in his tenure, not just for his approach to teaching but for his singing too. Even half a prompt or a modest audience was enough to bring a Talat Mahmood or a Manna Dey out of him. He had a talent no doubt; more importantly, he could pull out an apt song relevant to any mood or discussion and he sang from his heart. You could call him a walking juke box, requiring no coins!

Ouch! He Slapped the Hindi Teacher
August 5, 1980

DJ Singh was a 'hero.' He slapped the Hindi teacher. His defence? She inflicted cruelty on him.

Why did she do that? Because he could not recite a poem properly in Hindi, being half English from his mother's side. 'This is unfair,' he thought, 'that's why I am in school. To learn. She should teach me rather than get enraged.'

She hit him on the calves with a ruler and made him squat in a painful position for thirty minutes. Each time he stood to stretch himself, he was hit again. It got to him, and he hit back in a reflex action.

Of course, he was marched off to Br D'Souza. No one to date knows what transpired behind the closed doors of the headmaster's office.

Singing to the Pied Piper's Tunes
September 2, 1980

'An extract from the Pied Piper of Hamelin by Robert Browning', I announced, cranking up the decibels for the inter-class elocution competition. Followed by the recital of the famous poem by a group of twenty of us. I also called out 'Brown rats' when we reached the section:

... *And out of the houses the rats came tumbling.*
Great rats, small rats, lean rats, brawny rats,
Brown rats, black rats, grey rats, tawny rats ...

Our section fared poorly on the talent quotient and teachers had a tough time in getting a respectable creative output from us. But we sure surprised the elocution teacher, Mrs B Vander Holt, by lifting the trophy.

No one smelt a rat when the results were announced; we deserved the win.

The Showstopper Boys and 'Girls' of St. Columba's

Maharajas, soldiers, sheikhs, bandits, bridegrooms—the 'men' of our school were strutting all over town, showing off their queens, brides, Hawaiian dancers and 'vamps.' You could spot them in the posh Taj and Oberoi hotels, YMCA and even a conference of paediatricians. Who were these 'handsome men' and 'pretty ladies?'

The Muslim bride was Faiz Ahmed, the village bride was Sumit Malhotra, while Atul Sengupta was the groom whose bride had gone missing. The masquerade show was enacted by our junior schoolboys, choreographed by Br McPhilemy, Mrs Aimond and Mrs Bala.

The city found them adorable deserving standing ovations and thus invitations to various locations. Senior boys could not hold back the snickers, taking a dig at the gullible infants and yet jealous for the spreads the latter were treated to by each of their hosts.

'No Rules' Football Pitting Teachers Against Students
September 5, 1980

Two thousand students cheering their team, three dozen faculty looking on listlessly at theirs. It's Teachers' Day, when everything happens except … teaching. So why not a football game between the tutors and the boys?

It was the most chaotic game ever played on our grounds. Enthusiasm was aplenty, goals none till well into the second half. One lost count of the substitutions in Team Teachers; there was only so much stamina they had. Just when the boys seemed to be pressing on stronger, two lady teachers marched into the ground, tied the student goalie's hands behind his back and grabbed the whistle from the referee. From then on, it became a free-for-all. The whistle seemed to go off whenever boys had possession of the ball; after a while, no one was paying heed to anyone. It was raining goals, players shooting on both sides. Both sides claimed victory. An enterprising chap should have patented 'Freestyle Soccer', not as a sport but as theatre for entertainment.

The match was scheduled for Friday so teachers had the weekend to fix their muscular aches. To our disappointment, all of them reported to work on Monday.

Tantrum for an Expensive Pen, Lost It in a Day
October 14, 1980

I wanted a fountain pen. A relatively expensive one. I threw a tantrum at home. My mother finally relented and bought one. For me to lose it the following day itself.

We still lived in Kaka Nagar at the time—and had purchased the pen from Sunder Nagar market; the two localities were laid out on either side of Mathura Road. The brand was Teachers and its cost of Rs 25 was not minor by the standards of the time. I took it to school and walked around with it clipped to my shirt. It fell out sometime during the day, never to be seen again. I did not dare inform my mother.

Went back to writing with my old Camlin pens, hoping no one notices. My handwriting would not improve even when I was able to afford expensive pens in the future.

Couldn't We Reward Teachers with a Higher Remuneration?

Teachers were earning about Rs 1500 a month in the early to mid-eighties. Even if we consider cost of living then, it seemed like a pittance. How did they carry on? How did they stay so committed, working hard so we could earn well later?

Some gave private tuitions to supplement their incomes but not everyone had the temperament to. There were the street-smart ones too of course; they were running 'enterprises', setting up coaching centres. One had even engaged a fleet of buses to ferry the loads of students enrolled under him. But they were exceptions.

I learnt of the income of teachers long after I had graduated. I was doing well for myself by then but my heart wept thinking how they must have struggled to provide for their families. Could I give back to the generation of teachers whose contributions cannot be valued in monetary terms? Is it time for an endowment to provide for teachers who were not able to build a safety net for their later years?

Not all our faculty members are around anymore; a long time has passed since I was in school. But some are still out there who could do with a little help. There are also those who came in after we left; we could assist them in the memory of those who walked the school corridors in our time. They may not be seeking charity but could do with an opportunity to earn something even now. Honourably, as the only way they know.

How Do You Accommodate Two Kings on One Throne?

November 14, 1980

Our dramatics teacher, Mrs B. Vander Holt was in a fix—she had two kings and only one throne.

Varun Pawha was chosen for the role of king in the class play. But he fell sick a week before the performance and the throne lay vacant. Vikramjit Mukherjee was called in as an emergency replacement. He rose to the occasion, getting his lines and acting right. Only to leave the teacher facing a dilemma: Varun was back two days before the big day. Who would be king now? It would be unfair to drop either after the hard work they both put in. After all, the competition was on Children's Day and you could not have an unhappy boy.

A twist was added to the story. The king falls sick during the first act and resumes duty after the interval. Varun played king in the first half and Vikramjit during the second. Why did the king have to be unwell?

Varun was a heavier set boy. He 'loses weight' while sick, so the slimmer Vikramjit dons the royal robes after the interval. Innovative thinking, but we did not win the trophy!

You Do Not Miss School, Even If Slept for Two Hours!
December 5, 1980

My father woke my sister and me at six in the morning. To go to school. What was different that day? We had gone to sleep at four—we were out for a cousin's wedding. I assumed we would be allowed to bunk school having slept so late. But no such luck. Not only did I have to attend the classes but also stay back for a scout meeting. My mother had slept over at my aunt's home after the ceremonies but my father got us dressed and sent us off with our lunch.

In thirteen years of schooling, I did not miss a single class or a day of school unless I was home for medical reasons. Adults in school and home were strict disciplinarians; I may have grudged it then but its value is not lost on me now. That's why I can never get my head around those who skip school or work casually.

Mahatma Gandhi's Funeral: Once Again After Thirty-Three Years
January 31, 1981

It was a busy Saturday morning. We had to get ready and have breakfast before heading to India Gate for the 'funeral procession' of the father of the nation, Mahatma Gandhi. Exactly thirty three years after the actual cremation.

The occasion was the shooting of the film *Gandhi* by Richard Attenborough. The central vista of the city had been converted into a set—the deployment of 3,00,000 extras to show the mourning crowds would be entered into the Guinness Book of World Records. But did they really need to bring together all the extras? A shout-out would have brought enough people together anyway in a populated and curious country like India. The producers may not have wanted to take chances.

When we went to watch the movie in the cinema, I tried to find myself when we came to this scene. Of course, I could not.

Daylight Robbery: Black Kites Swooped Down for Our Lunch

It was mandatory to vacate the Middle School building during the break. Black Kites knew this and would circle in the hundreds over the field, eyeing our food. We had to either eat under a tree or hunch over while eating, covering the tiffin boxes with hands and arms. Yet, some of us lost our lunch to the swooping and stealing birds if we accidentally exposed our lunch boxes a second too long.

Without fail, some boys would tease these birds daily. They would tie a piece of bread at one end of a string and a scrap of paper at the other and leave it on the ground. It was just a matter of time before a bird picked the food and fly around with the paper a mini kite tagging along. Their 'tail' being picked up was a matter of achievement for the one who had planted it.

We called the birds Eagles in English incorrectly.

Last Minute Lecture Before Exam? Study It Well.
February 25, 1981

Why was Ms J. Vadehra insisting on extra classes to talk about the lives of Cezanne and Picasso just two days before the exam?

When studying at home, I ignored both these lessons, my reasoning being how important could it be as a last minute thing? Turns out the exam papers had been prepared with two questions on these artists and Ms Vadehra had to cover these no matter what. I did badly in the paper and felt a dunce for my illogical reasoning.

Cezanne and Picasso were also her last lectures in St. Columba's—she left soon after and we never heard of her again. Many a boy would miss her since she was considered a work of art in herself by many. Ajay Khanna and Deepak D'Souza were her favourites, helping them hone their natural talents; they attained meritorious positions at various competitions. They definitely rued the going away of their mentor. We were not taught art after class five.

Time is Over ... in the Library

There was a time when we had to be pushed out of the library—who could have thought there would be a day when people would have to be pushed in? Schools do send their students to the library but increasingly it seems taking a horse into the library to read books would be easier.

We looked forward to the library period to borrow from a vast selection. Close to the bell going off, the Middle School librarian Mrs I.J. Mohinder would announce, 'Tiiiiiimmmmmeeeee is overrrrr ... ' in a distinct tone, dragging the vowels. Perched on a highchair, her voice resonated across the room and we would rush to get books issued in time. Her distinct tone has stayed etched in our memories for life.

The library was an important place for our education and entertainment. Not just the one in school but any we could access. Until the third standard, the Government ran the Delhi Public

Library bus which used to come weekly to our neighbourhood for us to borrow a book. There was another walking distance from school in the Bhai Vir Sahitya Sadan where I read many comics for free. I was fortunate to have access to the Delhi Gymkhana Club library, one of the best even to date.

And then there was the friends and family library—where we freely borrowed from each other, fully aware many books are unlikely to come back. In class six, I set up a library at home. We collected books from all children in the neighbourhood—the two cartons full were a gold mine to read from. Books mattered to us. They shaped who we have become.

Unfortunately, time is over for many a library and its patrons!

Entered Class Six

April 2, 1981

We moved up literally—to class 6-D located on the first floor. Mid way through the year and we would have completed half of our K-12 education. Ms N. Gill, the one of a cheerful demeanour, would be our class teacher. Her happy state could be attributed to being in love!

Mrs Robinson Retires

April 6, 1981

Mrs Marie Robinson retired after twenty-three years of service—teaching students of class one. Including me in 1976.

We got to know only after she had left school; I wish all those who had been taught by her had been invited to bid her a goodbye. And to express our gratitude. The tradition could have been established for all teachers leaving school.

It is a moment to also recall all the class teachers I had. Mrs Aimond, Mrs Robinson, Mrs Monica Singh, Mrs Nazareth, Mrs Wintle, Mrs Das, Ms Gill, Mrs Vaid, Mr Innis, Br Fernandes and Mr Peter Rocha—— they were there in this order from kindergarten to twelfth. Thank you for making a part of me just like you.

Charlie Needed a Break. Thus, Sent to Clean Playground.

July 7, 1981

We came back from break for the Science class but just would not settle down. The fifty of us were at our unruly worst, talking incessantly and sending flying missiles across the classroom. No problem. If an extended recess was what we sought, then that's what we would be granted. We were sent back to the playground—not to frolic but to scavenge.

On a hot and humid day, we were ordered to pick every piece of garbage on the ground—no mean task after a herd of 1,000 boys spent their break there. Pickings including dry paper, food dropping, ketchup and jam laden wrappers, bottle caps, even tissue with snot. We would not be allowed back till every scrap had been removed.

We sobered up for a few weeks at least. We did not want to be sent back to pick the filth of others with our bare hands.

Why couldn't we just have been caned on our backsides instead?

Parents, Stay Out. Let Teachers Educate Your Child.

Why did St. Columba's attract the best of teachers? Because they were trusted and empowered to do what they were meant to: educate us.

Parents had little say in the matter. They were allowed through the gates only when report cards were handed out by the class teacher and progress of their boys discussed. There was no interference allowed otherwise. Their job was to focus on our upbringing at home.

The school management always stood behind its staff; they were respected for dedicating their lives to a noble profession. Only then were teachers able to command the same respect from boys and their parents. That is how you built the ideal ethos and value system of the institution, further imbibed in us through osmosis and instruction. So, we may further be a positive influence wherever life takes us.

Frank Hardy is Dead
August 20, 1981

Just when I thought I had read the complete *Hardy Boys* series, Rajnish Walia mentioned he's got the latest in which Frank, one of the detective brother duo, dies. I had never heard of it and could not find it in any library or bookshop. 'It's not come to India but I managed to get one through an aunt coming from the USA,' he claimed.

Each time I asked if I could borrow it, he would reply in the affirmative—but always in hushed tones as if dealing in contraband. He never delivered; in fact, he never even brought the book when I asked to at least see it.

Seems like this edition was a figment of Rajnish's imagination and he was just seeking attention. Frank never died but my trust in Rajnish's words did.

Selected in Two Sports Teams. Dropped From Both.
September 12, 1981

I made it to two class sports teams on a single day of trials—only to be dropped from both within twenty-four hours.

Mr Tommy Lockwood selected me for the cricket team on the basis of how I held the bat to play a defensive shot—I just had to pose, no one bowled to me. But when I actually took to the field for a practice session, others realized I was not going to win any matches for them.

I was also selected as a goalkeeper of the hockey team—but my name was scratched without anyone consulting me. To date, I have no idea who took the decision and what the basis for it was.

The Hots for Mrs Sudon
1981-82

An extra-terrestrial force seemed to follow whichever classroom Mrs Rebecca Sudon entered. Boys in the front rows 'accidentally' keep dropping pencils and other objects in rapid succession—a phenomena occurring only in Mrs Sudon's class. Was there an explanation for this?

There was no external force, only dirty minds at play. Objects would be dropped so boys could bend to pick them up—keeping their eyes glued in the teacher's direction. Towards her legs if one wants to be more specific. Because she wore skirts to school and sat with her legs crossed. Anything for a viewing!

It seems all the boys in school had the hots for her—some male teachers too. Rumour was she had the hots for Shahrukh Khan, still a middle school student at St. Columba's. There was unlikely to be any truth in this but SRK's public relations machinery was already cranking up his charm long before he became the heartthrob of the nation.

When we learnt she was going to be teaching us, we could not hide our glee. Our seniors readily shared tips on how to get the best sightings. There was a scramble to grab the front row seats but what followed was anti-climactic. She walked in, not in a skirt but a long maternity dress. No pencils would fall that day, only our faces. Within three months, she left to deliver her baby, never to return.

Cutting Up National Geographic for Love
October 6, 1981

Who cuts up National Geographic magazines?

Mr Burrett, Geography teacher for classes nine and ten, brought a stack of Nat Geos, cutting out relevant images for a project initiated by our class teacher Ms Gill. Publications like those came at a premium and its customers were likely to archive them for the timelessness of their content. So it was a surprise when we were given some to clip images of animals, birds, insects and marine life.

The reasons for this generosity would become clear later. Mr Burrett was either dating or wooing Ms Gill; they would go on to get married the following year.

School Uniform: The Leveller

We pray to Maa Lakshmi, the goddess of wealth, every Diwali, the date falling sometime in October or November. If there was one business on whom the Goddess always smiled was Devi Lal's.

He had a quasi-monopoly stitching winter uniforms for many schools including ours. Most of us needed a new set of trousers and blazers; we were growing boys, so sizes changed rapidly. Given our antics, uniforms suffered from wear and tear requiring them to be discarded every season. Orders were placed around Diwali, marking the onset of winter in north India.

We had to adhere strictly to prescribed fabrics and colours and getting from Devi Lal's was a safe bet. Not that it was mandatory; we could choose any vendor. All of us were thus sporting attire cut from the same cloth—irrespective of our social and economic status. A great leveller no doubt.

Overconfidence is a Snake Bite
November 9, 1981

I usually got an A in Composition—that's what essay writing was called. It got to my head. When the next assignment came, I wrote smug in the knowledge of always doing well, only to end up with a C.

We had discussed snake bites in class and were asked to write about a situation when someone is attacked by a snake. Why did I get a C? In my essay, I identified the bites on the victim to be non-poisonous. However, the follow-up steps I described were relevant only if the venom could kill. The storyline was entirely off-track.

Whenever I feel cocky, I remind myself of the snake bite to ground myself and apply myself to the task at hand with humility.

Bal Mela: A Grand Fete, Raising Money for Many a Cause
November 14, 1981

The annual Bal Mela (Children's Fete) is a day we all looked forward to—held on November 14, the birthday of former

Prime Minister and a founding father of independent India, Jawaharlal Nehru. Celebrated nationally as Children's Day.

As usual, the Junior School grounds had scores of stalls selling street food, toys, clothes and knick-knacks at bargain prices. It's the games where I spent maximum time, trying my luck at Lucky Dip, Lucky 7 and Tambola. There were rides too, most popular being the ones on the elephant, permissible in those days.

What happened to the money raised on the day? It went to causes the school thought could do with a contribution, however modest. Some of the beneficiaries for this year were:

Leprosy Patients Hospital: Rs 2,000
Sisters of the Destitute: Rs 4,900
St. George's Free School Calcutta: Rs 10,000
Low Income Family Emancipation Society: Rs 600
Poor Boys O.L. School Dadar: Rs 1,000
Mother Theresa Missionaries: Rs 8,000
C. B. Rehabilitation Centre, Calcutta: Rs 10,000
Cheshire Homes: Rs 3,000
Sisters of the Destitute: Rs 1,865
Kanhai Harijans: Rs 1,000
Mentally Retarded Society: Rs 2,000
Ozanam Home: Rs 3,000
Prabhat Rohtak: Rs 2,000
Sweaters for poor boys: Rs 386
Khrist Raja School: Rs 1,000
St. John's Boys' Home Khera Khurd: Rs 3,000

Little Flower Vincent de Paul (Kingsway Camp): Rs 1,000
Nutrition for Balwadi Jehangirpuri: Rs 1,000
Balwadi (Fr. Vincent): Rs 5,000
Poor boys St. Vincent School, Asansol: Rs 500
Institution for the Blind, Panchkuin Road: Rs 1,000
Sisters of the Destitute: Rs 1,200
Khrisi Raj School: Rs 1,000
Poor Boys Bassein: Rs 1,000
St. Mary's (C.B.) Orphanage Calcutta: Rs 10,000
St. Paul's Poor Tamil Catholics: Rs 1,000

The Promise of Good Karma Does Not Sell Raffle Tickets

At least once a year, we would be assigned the task of selling raffle tickets to raise money for charity. Costing between Re 1 to Rs 5. The draw would be made during the annual Bal Mela.

I would go door to door in the neighbourhood, in the afternoons—a tactic any sales manual would warn you against. Aunties, and the rest of their household, woken up from their afternoon siesta would not find a stranger boy endearing, more so if he is asking for money for a cause they had no relation to. Of course they declined, with all the politeness they could muster up while spanking me hard in their minds.

On one occasion a child opened the door, told me her mother could not get up—so I went in to try to sell the ticket to a medically impaired bedridden woman. She did not believe good karma will bring her relief and turned me away.

Eventually my father would buy some tickets as a face-saver for me.

A Class Monitor with Charlie in His Hands Can Run Amok
November 26, 1981

Power corrupts. A class monitor allowed the use of a rod can make him vile.

I was appointed one in class six—and I assumed the authority of a teacher. No one could get away by chatter and mischief under my watch—I promptly struck them with my wooden ruler. For the smallest of infractions, I would snitch on my classmates to Ms Gill. Linus Gomes got an earful when he was reported for spitting in the bathroom; I did not mention it was in the wash basin, not the walls or the floor.

The boys started complaining about the excesses I was committing; Ms Gill had to finally dismiss me. And forbade the use of a Charlie by any monitor henceforth.

The humiliation would pass. Another lesson in exercise and retention of power would stay embedded.

Charlie Gets Very Upset When You Score Two in Sanskrit
January 6, 1982

Br D'Souza barged in holding a sheet of paper. 'Varun Pawha,' he called out. Varun stepped up and received four whacks. 'That's what you get for scoring two, yes two, out of hundred in the Sanskrit exam. Rohit Srivastava,' out he called the next name after. Whoosh, whoosh, whoosh, whoosh—for scoring six.

Sanskrit marks did not count in our overall percentage and rank, so studying it felt pointless and torturous. We despised the subject now, the teacher Mrs Handa even more so. Rohit would say he suffered public humiliation at its worst because of her. He could have saved himself from it: by being attentive in class and preparing well for the exams.

If Half My Class Were Girls ...

You would expect all of us to root for girls being admitted to St. Columba's, but there was no unanimity to be found on the matter. On hindsight, I would stick to going to an all-boys institution.

As a fun exercise, a bunch of sixth graders were asked about the prospect of half their class being girls. Two contrasting replies stood out:

'If half my class were girls, I would like the best of them and would not let anybody else set an eye on her. I hope that the girls would think of me as the smartest boy in the class and would always be after me. We would sit together in the library and talk about the good books there. I would have a nice time in school.' - Rahul Bhayana

'It would certainly be a nightmare if half my class were girls. I would feel awful with some giggly girls sitting all around me, especially if one of them was my partner. Any boy would really feel very embarrassed if he is punished in front of the girls. A girl would probably start crying if she got a beating from any teacher. The toughest part would be the swimming period. And when we queue up for drinking water from the cooler, the prefects would say ladies first and the poor boys would have to stand right at the back. In the break, the girls would sit down talking about latest fashions, make-up things, while the boys would be busy playing hand cricket or other games. I DON'T LIKE GIRLS IN MY CLASS! - Nitin Pasricha

A Cricket Kit for Mr Burrett
January 16, 1982

Mr Burrett was in a fix. He had scheduled a friendly cricket match between the staff of St. Columba's and of Frank Anthony Public School, his former employer. At the last minute, Br Farrell declined the use of the kit. After all the efforts to bring the teams together, Mr Burrett was caught in a potentially embarrassing situation.

That's where you relied upon Br D'Souza to play Superman. He pulled out a wad of cash from his pocket, had someone go across to the sports stores of nearby Connaught Place and return with more than was required including four gleaming bats and six menacing red leather balls.

Who won? Every won!

1982: Br C.F. O'Farrell Completes Fifty Years as a Christian Brother

Half a century ago, Br C.F. O'Farrell answered the call of his vocation—taking up teaching assignments at schools and colleges run by the Christian Brotherhood. A significant part of his career had been at St. Columba's—generations of students should count it as their good fortune! How do people like him defy their age and keep going with unwavering commitment and infinite enthusiasm?

His forte may have been mathematics, but he was known to study physics and chemistry late into the night—to be able to lend help to those requiring additional academic assistance. If any other teacher needed a role model to emulate, they need not have looked beyond Br O'Farrell.

His body was no less agile than his mind. Rookie coach to the school team, he could send anyone scurrying on the tennis court with his stamina and range of shots. And remind students they had mountains to climb before they could claim to be masters themselves.

Necks Bent for Rubik's Cube and Video Games

It would be a quarter of a century before humanity at large would be spotted with necks bent, looking at something glowing in their palms. The Rubik's Cube and pocket video games were a harbinger of what lay in store.

Take the Rubik's Cube. Like the rest of the world, Columbans too were obsessed with solving the puzzle in the fastest time possible. Ravi Sankrit and Manish Sinha set a school record of doing it in fifty six seconds. I could never figure the logic behind it—the best I would manage was getting all colours on one of the faces.

Video games were the other craze. Nintendo popularized pocket-sized games under the 'Game & Watch' brand and anyone who knew someone coming from overseas was getting these. I got two—Donkey Kong and Fire—from Qatar. Casio digital watches gained in popularity too—they came loaded with games you played with micro buttons. Even those with pudgy fingers managed.

These fads lasted longer than some others, marked by people standing, sitting or walking around with heads titled forward. Keeping at it despite sore thumbs and strained eyes.

Rajat Khanna Passes Away
March 25, 1982

Rajat Khanna, one of sweetest amongst us, passed away when he fell ill on a scout trip to Dalhousie, contracting bronchial pneumonia. An enthusiastic boy scout, he punched above his relatively shorter height and fragility. Every heart in the school wept for him.

His twin Lalit, also in our batch, was always seen as the 'big brother' looking out for the sibling. We wondered how he coped with the loss, never being able to take his eyes off the vacuum in the classroom, never to be filled?

Entered Class Seven

April 5, 1982

I could see a swagger in everyone' body language—this is the class year when we would enter our teens, giving us that grown-up feeling. It would also be an enjoyable time with Mrs Anita Vaid, our class teacher, who joined the school recently. She may have been the mother of one our batchmates, Rohit, but came across as a fun-seeking college student. Class 7-D, here come the teens!

This is the year when Br R.B. Oman retired as our principal, Br J.P. Pinto taking his place.

An Open Letter to the New Principal

1982

How do you share your expectations from the incoming principal? Not easy on his face, more so if Charlie is always with him, twitching for action in a new set of hands. So, the editors of the school magazine carried an open letter to the incoming principal, 'Bro' J.P. Pinto. Cheeky. Here is an extract, typographical errors deliberately retained:

> *Dear Sir,*
> *PLEASE:*
>
> 1. *Do believe in the fact that little drops make an ocean – give a holiday everytime it rains.*

2. *Do believe in the saying "Practice makes perfect" – let us practice during class hours.*
3. *Do let us go and see every match our school team plays – of course, only if it is during class hours.*
4. *Do hold all staff meetings during class hours. Our teachers would get a well deserved rest. So would we.*
5. *Don't get het up and bothered every time you see a prankster at work – the youth energy is being given vent to.*
6. *Don't walk around to the classes to check happenings – a boy rudely awakened from slumber can be badly shocked.*
7. *Don't wonder what you had done that God had decided to punish you by making you Principal of a school with about 3000 pranksters – He did have a reason.*

Teaching a Lesson to Campa Cola Thief
April 14, 1982

If you saw Rahul Dass coming your way, you downed your Campa Cola in one go or scampered away out of his sight. Because he would request for a sip from yours and empty out three quarters of the bottle. Considering them close friends, he invariably sought Badal Gulati and Varun Pawha out to 'share their drink with him.'

It got to Badal one day and he decided to teach Rahul a lesson. He went to a crate with discarded bottles, collecting the remains at the bottom of each into one bottle till it was nearly full to the top. He got Varun to spit in it and he did too. When they spotted Rahul, they pretended to jostle for the drink.

As was his style, Rahul casually asked for a swig—the other two willingly obliged, as good friends should. For a change, Rahul consumed all of it. But Badal had to rub it in: he told Rahul what he had drunk.

'No way, you are kidding,' said Rahul, in that tone of denial when someone hears bad news. Badal swore it was the truth, Varun nodded in agreement supressing a grin. Rahul still refused to believe them. Then and forever. What you don't see, you don't accept, hence it did not happen.

When We Found the Government Napping in Parliament
April 27, 1982

We studied Civics in school, so why not visit the Parliament to witness lawmakers in action? Passes were arranged for our class to visit the Lok Sabha, the lower House, to attend a session in the afternoon. Only for us to find the Government napping. Literally.

There were barely seventy members, just above the quorum mark for the session to be held. Most seemed to be sleeping. Mr P.A. Sangma, Minister of State for Commerce, was droning on with no one seemingly paying attention. The deputy speaker of the house, Mr G. Lakshmanan, was officiating; he must be on a special drug to be able to stay awake himself.

Entering the Parliament was a rare experience but did little to inspire confidence in the state of affairs.

Summers Be Like …

The onset of summers meant switching from warm grey trousers to white cotton ones and mothballing our blazers and sweaters.

The summer is long in north India, and it felt even further stretched because all we had were fans—placebos to make us feel cool. Electric supply was erratic and there were no generators. Windows were thus left open to let the "climate" in, as the poor joke went. Seats along the windows were sought after in the summers and avoided in winters. The bus ride back in the afternoon was not comfortable either; the 'loo' breeze would pierce like needles through windows that would not close and doors that did not exist.

It got particularly bad when we were out for hours practising for Sports Day or just playing games, with no immediate access to drinking water. Mr Burrett had a formula to beat the heatstroke: drink as much water as your belly could hold. Feel heavy but only for a while. It kept thirst and dehydration at bay.

Signs of summer and humid monsoons were all around us. The sweat patches on the saree blouses of lady teachers. Shirts of men too. Our white shirts camouflaged the moist bits, but we could smell each other, unavoidable, considering the time spent in close proximity of one another. Deodorants were unheard of, talcum powder had limited effectiveness. We were always thirsty—queuing up at water coolers whenever allowed to. Cupping our hands under the faucet to drink, filling our bottles and dousing our hair and faces with the cool water.

But hell, we were never uncomfortable. It was life and we never cribbed.

'Mummy, Save Me From Charlie!'
July 6, 1982

'Yogi, has your mummy come?'

Everyone was asking Yogi the whereabouts of his mother. Why? While being caned the previous day, he had squealed 'mummmmyyyy' for everyone in the class to hear. Word spread. His backside was red with the six whacks, his face redder with indignation.

Mukul Dev Kaushal, his co-conspirator, received eight instead of six—because he found Yogi's cry amusing. 'You find this entertaining, right? Let's give you an extra two so you can laugh more,' said the headmaster.

Not that is mattered to Mukul; so often was he asked to bend over that he seemed to have developed an immunity to the pain. 'Bring it on' could well be his war cry!

Colour. And Movies. In Our Living Room!
April 25, 1982

Just like that, overnight, many shades of grey went out of our lives. On April 25, 1982, the state run television service,

Doordarshan, a monopoly at the time, started airing in colour.

A few companies were given licences to manufacture television sets and partial liberalisation allowed imports too. Despite the relatively low purchasing power of the rupee and modest income levels, millions found the money to invest in colour televisions. The cost of one was equivalent to a few months' salary of a teacher. New Delhi was hosting the Asian Games for the second time since the inaugural edition in 1950; a condition to awarding the right to host was having infrastructure for live telecast of the games in colour. Thus, the modernisation of broadcast infrastructure began.

Doordarshan upped its game in content so there was more to watch than the drab fare we had to grudgingly accept; to their credit, they commissioned programs hooking the nation with their production quality and storylines. A welcome change for a nation not getting more than the Sunday movie and myriad Bollywood based entertainment like *Chitrahaar* and *Phool Khile Hain Gulshan Gulshan*.

Parallelly, the VCR or the Video Cassette Recorder, also made an entry. A new industry in home entertainment boomed. Shops renting out compatible VHS tapes sprouted. No one complained about the quality of images and sound as pirated versions and multiple copies from a master, were circulated. Standard rental was Rs 10 a day. New releases could be had for only three hours as the next customer was waiting. What if the producers did not release a VHS version of their films? Don't discount the inventiveness of Indians. They made camera prints: by pointing a video camera at the screening of a film in a theatre and making multiple copies. The images were dull, the sound muffled but customers did not care. People were hosting movie parties, sometimes to show off their swanky equipment.

Columbans—like most other adolescent boys of the time—were getting together to watch porn from the West. Movies were rated single, double and triple X. Tapes were being exchanged in the classroom surreptitiously. The VCR certainly moved the needle in the moral compass and hastened sexual liberation in India, even if a majority continued to be prudes.

My father picked up a job in 1982 requiring him to make trips to the Middle-East almost every month for nearly a decade. On each trip, he would be doing someone a favour by bringing back a television set or a VCR. Even after paying customs duties, you were getting better products at a cheaper price than those available locally. Given the sizeable south Asian population and dearth of cinemas, VHS versions of movies from India reached the region much sooner than back home. He would bring these back for us and as gifts for others.

Running VCRs From South-East Asia

Mr Mavely was one of the teachers organizing overseas trips for students to supplement his income. He not only made money from selling the package, but by 'running VCRs' too.

Anyone returning from overseas was allowed duty free imports only up to a certain value, the levies very high beyond this. Mr Mavely purchased one VCR per student with him and had them declare it as part of their baggage respectively. He paid the duties, collected the VCRs when outside the airport and sold them at a juicy profit later. The trips were thus to Malaysia, Thailand and Singapore—attractive for tourists and amongst the cheapest to buy electronics from.

Nothing illegal in what he did! Did the principal know about this?

Br J.A. Macphilemy: An Emotional Farewell
July 28, 1982

All teachers respected him, the ladies amongst them loved him too. Little boys adored him, while their mothers all but swooned in his presence. If he had been in Hollywood, he could have been a bad boy, but he chose to be Brother J.A. Macphilemy: Vice principal of the school and headmaster of the Junior School for twelve years.

A farewell befitting his stature and in appreciation for what he had done, could not be modest even if he himself was in every sense of the word. Reams of golden paper transformed the foyer of the Junior School into a place of beauty. The cafeteria was decorated with flowers and buntings, the Cathedral looked heavenly adorned with exquisite posies.

Mass was followed by theatre—not that Br Macphilemy had not seen enough drama during his time at the school. Curtains went up for *Alibaba and the Forty Thieves* enacted by junior classes, a riot act if there was one. Followed by a lavish lunch catered by the upscale Claridges hotel, a meal to be savoured and talked about for a long time to come.

A written tribute by a teacher, unsigned, summed up what Brother meant to us. An extract (as appeared in the original text):

To every one of those thousands of little boys who have been through the Junior School over these years, you were a friend, a guide, a doctor, someone whose hands were eminently clingable. Even the boys who entered your office in order to be reprimanded, left it in a quieter mood, but still as friends. It was a great pleasure to see the little boys filing into your office to get 'very pleased' signed on their copies. More touching still, to see them return with sweets produced from some secret 'khazana' which evidently was always overstocked. I often wonder whether it was the signature or the sweets that attracted them to your office.

A typical day in your life saw you tearing up and down the corridors, entering the classrooms (sometimes on all fours) to pep up the sometimes waning spirit, racing across the fields to get something for the little boy who lost his tiffin box; doing it all in what seemed to be in a trice.

Break-time was playing with the boys, kicking the ball all over the field, everywhere, except the goal. A cut, a broken tooth, a bruise, a gash; these were some of the more run-of-the-mill surgical complaints that you attended to each day.

It makes one tired just looking at the pace at which you operate, but then, that's what makes you marvellous. So now you're going, and a teacher remembers all that Brother Mac has done for me. 'Taught me the power of prayer, love for the poor. Taught me to speak well of others, to leave hurtful things unspoken. Now go bouncing with life and energy like a spring chicken. Carrying on the good work. Passing it on.'

Continue like Paul, being 'all things to all men.' It works. Believe me. It does.

The School is Not a Travel Agency!
August 10, 1982

No one is going to Singapore or Germany.

Two different teachers were selling trips to these countries; they did so sometimes to supplement their income and the school would permit it. But not when it becomes a fish market.

Overseas travel was a luxury few could afford and both "travel agents" got down to a slugfest to lure customers to themselves. By offering discounts, putting each other down and taking students and parents aside to hard sell.

The teachers forgot they were in St. Columba's School and Br D'Souza reminded them. By withdrawing permission. All future trips were subject to strict scrutiny.

Learning Secularism in a Christian Missionary School

Why would anyone leave the comforts and security of the western world, settle in a difficult region like India, driven to teach generations of boys; unruly and docile, bright and dim, rich and poor?

How can you look at such men with suspicion, doubting their intent, questioning their motives? They are guided by their religion but they do not impose it upon others. Not once in thirteen years was Christianity, or any other religion, discussed in the classroom. Not once were we asked to offer prayers in the Sacred Heart Cathedral, one of the most important churches in India, standing between St. Columba's and Convent of Jesus and Mary.

Ours was a truly secular environment, in letter and in spirit. Christian boys were taken to Catechism classes while others stayed back for Moral Science. To be taught what it means to be a conscientious citizen of this planet, a good human in society.

The years following independence were quite liberal and then the mood and narrative started changing politically. Things were progressively made more difficult for Irish brothers running St. Columba's and for other western missionaries. Each was projected as being here to convert our population to Christianity, while all they wanted was for us to be proficient in mathematics, english, science, tennis and other subjects and sports. Upholding the right principles, with empathy and charity towards all.

They carried on, standing tall on pillars of truth and justice, even if vilified by those who saw them as missionaries out to change our demography. They were here to uplift anyone who needed to be; it did not matter whether they prayed to Ram, Allah or Jesus, or to no one in particular.

Those who were in the country would stay on but entry was restricted to new ones coming in. Leaving our country poorer, being denied education and a value system agnostic of ethnicity and religion. Because these Brothers not only taught us but brought the best out in other teachers.

The Day Amitabh Bachchan 'Died'
July 25, 1982

Scene: A star is declared clinically dead. There is mass hysteria across the nation, millions praying for his recovery. The wife is by his side, clenching her holy book, not averting her gaze for even a moment lest she miss out on any sign of life. And then is there one, the slightest one: the toe moves. She screams out to the doctors, pleading they not give up yet. And they don't. Eventually the man in intensive care opens his eyes. To keep going strong for decades to come.

We have seen similar scenes in movies any number of times but here was a case of fact being stranger than fiction. Amitabh Bachchan was injured while shooting on the sets of *Coolie*, a result of not relying on body doubles for stunts. A mild pain initially turned out to be severe intestinal rupture and he had to be rushed from Bangalore to Bombay for treatment. For days, the doctors struggled to save him before the miracle in Breach Candy Hospital made medical history.

It would take Amitabh Bachchan months to find his strength after multiple surgeries. He would be back to work in just over five months, *Coolie* emerging the top grosser of 1983. It was the last time any of his movies with him in the lead would finish at the top, although he did belt out a few more blockbusters. Not that he would fade away. He would adapt for both television and the big screen, his face ubiquitous in the lives of Indians even in his eighties.

Ashamed in Swimming Competition
August 10, 1982

The inter-class swimming competitions were on and I signed up for the fifty metre relay team; I was selected because only three other boys stepped up for a team of four.

I was up against Amit Talwar, who wore braces in his legs, having been afflicted with polio as an infant. 'Him I can beat,' I boasted in my mind. When it was our turn, he dived, I jumped—I cannot dive even now—and we were off. I completed the first lap of the twenty five metres long pool and turned around for the second. I looked back to see where Amit was, but he was nowhere in sight. I looked in front and there he was—fifteen metres ahead, almost at the finish line. It was a no-competition between us.

He may have been differently abled in his leg but I was in my thinking. I continued swimming till the end, ashamed, humbled and defeated.

Revenge Time: Hitting Br D'Souza With a Hockey Stick
September 3, 1982

'You hit me because I caned you last week?'

That was Br D'Souza confronting Sourish Mitra on the hockey field during a game between students and staff to mark Teacher's Day. Sourish's hockey stick struck Br D'Souza on the shin, in what would normally have been seen as a hazard of the game. But the headmaster was not 'Superman' without reason; he remembered everything, connecting dots instantly. He caned scores of boys every week, each incident stored photographically in his brain; he knew Sourish was taking his 'revenge.'

Sourish felt ashamed at the look Br D'Souza gave him and yet pleaded innocence, admitting only later it was deliberate. Ouch!

Presenting Shahrukh Khan: As the Wiz
November 26, 1982

Everyone wanted a ticket to *The Wiz*—because it was our first major theatrical production after *SMIKE* and Shahrukh Khan was in the lead. I made my reservations too, only to fall sick.

There was a strange virus in town and half the school seemed to have been affected for over two months. Just when I thought I had been spared, I succumbed as amongst the last to. The timing could not have been worse. I went missing in the class photo—the only year I would not figure in the school magazine. And my tickets to *The Wiz* went waste.

Perhaps the most popular of all productions by the school to date, the adaptation of *The Wizard of Oz* was a musical opera never to be forgotten by those who attended. Many a student became a star overnight. Palash Sen—who would go on to form the band *Euphoria*—as the Tin Man, and Kaustav Mitra as sweet Dorothy stood out with Shahrukh as the eccentric, unapproachable Wiz himself.

Anshuman Swami, the very droll cowardly Lion and Rajinder Bhattacharya, the loose-limbed cheeky scarecrow, impressed no less. And there were the cameos by the most realistic looking 'Witches of the East and West,' The Mice (sic) squad, the Poppies, the Winkies, and the Munchkins—each striking and visually appealing. Music by Rocky Fernandes was the masterstroke. How did Br D'Souza manage the cast of over 150 students, getting the best out of them?

The primary goals—that of raising funds for the school's computer and the Teacher's Benefit Fund—were achieved in excess of projections. Columbans certainly had something to crow about for years to come!

The Songs We Sung

Picnics and trips would be occasions for dozens of boys to sing together – and a few favourites became anthemic to us. It did not matter whether you knew the lyrics completely or not or you were in sync or not. The spirit mattered. Extracts from some ...

SONG 1

If I were a bachelor, and if I were to marry,
 I would want a carpenter's daughter more than any other.
 So I could screw, and she could screw, and we could screw together,
 From late at night to early morn, screwing one another.

In the morning, in the morning, in the morning by the sea,
In the morning, in the morning, in the morning by the sea.
The song goes on with the carpenter being replaced with, say, a vampire so you could suck together or a dentist so you could drill together. We just kept inventing as we sang.

SONG 2: By Harry Belafonte

All day, all night, Mary Ann
Down by the seaside siftin' sand
Even little children love Mary Ann
Down by the seaside siftin' sand.
Mary Ann, Oh, Mary Ann
Oh, won't you marry me?
We can have a bamboo hut
With brandy in the tea
Leave your fat old mama home
She never will say yes
If your mama don't know now
She can guess.

SONG 3

Jack and Jill went up the hill
To fetch a pail of water
God knows what they did up there
But they came down with a daughter.

SONG 4

She'll be coming around the mountain when she comes (when she comes) - Repeat
    She'll be coming around the mountain - Repeat
    She'll be coming around the mountain when she comes

    Singing aye aye yippee yippee aye (Yee-haw) - Repeat
    Singing aye aye yippee
    Aye aye yippee
    Aye aye yippee yippee aye

    She'll be driving six white horses when she comes (Giddy up!)
    She'll be driving six white horses when she comes (Giddy up!)

SONG 5: Shame and scandal in the family by Shawn Elliott

> In Trinidad there was a family
> With much confusion as you will see
> It was a mama and a papa and a boy who was grown
> He wanted to marry, have a wife of his own
> Found a young girl that suited him nice
> Went to his papa to ask his advice
> His papa said: 'Son, I have to say no,
> This girl is your sister, but your mama don't know.'

SONG 6: My Ding-a-Ling by Chuck Berry

When I was a little biddy boy
My grandmother bought me a cute little toy
Silver bells hanging on a string
She told me it was my ding-a-ling-a-ling
My Ding-A-Ling My Ding-A-Ling I want you to play with My Ding-A-Ling (Repeat)
This here song it ain't so sad
The cutest little song you ever had
Those of you who will not sing
You must be playing with your own Ding-a-ling.

SONG 7: We Shall Overcome ...

Every boy in Junior School was trained to sing this song in a group, and even those with a voice like mine had to participate. Maybe the music teacher thought, I too, shall overcome my music handicap:
Hum Honge Kaamyab, Hum Honge Kaamyab
Hum Honge Kaamyab Ek Din
Oh maan Mein Hai Viswash, Pura Hai Viswash
Hum Honge Kaamyab Ek Din.
The English version goes, 'We shall overcome one day ... '

Pakistan Beats India 7-1; No One Wants to Play Hockey

December 2, 1982

The trials to select teams for inter-class hockey tournaments were on but there was a problem. Most sections could not muster up eleven players to take the field, forget having a choice of players.

India had been hammered by traditional rivals Pakistan, seven goals to one, the previous day in the finals of the Asian Games, and that too as hosts—a low after winning the Olympics gold two years ago in Moscow. The demoralisation was showing at the trials.

Trust Br D'Souza to summon his superpowers. He called up reserves for matches starting the following week: Antonio Pacheco, Joe Chirayath, M. Mavely, T. Palamattam and others made up for the shortfall in squads. Who were they? Teachers at ease in shorts, reasonably fit, lest sore muscles keep them away from work and able to wield a stick without breaking anyone's leg (or their own).

Watching their teachers play the first round enthused enough boys to turn up with their sticks for subsequent matches and sending the reserves back to writing on the blackboard.

Anish 'Memorises' Just by Reading Everything Three Times Over
January 4, 1983

'If you read all course work three times over, you will be well prepared for the exams. No need to tax your brain to memorise. And it will save so much time.'

Anish Tawakley found this to be one hell of an advice from Gurpreet Singh, and tried it for the mid-term exams. With spectacular results. His scores fell by over 20 per cent.

That's what happens when you pay heed to someone who's always scored less than you. Anish would not forget this lesson and went back to the tried and tested method of learning by rote. He managed to restore his grades in the finals.

The First, And Last, Day of My Tennis Career
January 15, 1983

I was still looking for a sport to find fame in. Tennis might be it—considering not too many boys were seen playing it. I set up a time to play with Ajay Khanna on the school's concrete court.

We had knocked around for barely ten minutes when Br Farrel walked in. Without even making eye contact, he brushed the two of us aside to play with his partner. That's it—no request, no apology, no come-back-later. We were flies on the court, swatted away.

My enthusiasm for the game lay punctured. I hung up my racquet, for good. On the day my tennis career started and ended.

I Called Our Teacher Sexy—Others Could Not Get Over It!
March 25, 1983

Walking back from the last exam of class seven, I was thinking of the class teacher—she had come in jeans and a T-shirt and was sporting plaits on either side of her head. Looking very different from her usual self.

'Ma'am was looking quite sexy,' I remarked to Joel Fernandes on the way to the bus. Joel looked at me in utter disbelief and then started telling others out loud, repeatedly, 'Oh man, Ajay Jain has used the word sexy ... would you believe it?'

Was a goody-too-shoes reputation a useful one to have had? Maybe not. Because then others don't invite you to join in the 'fun' considering me a misfit!

Entered Class Eight. And the Digital World.
April 4, 1983

The last year before the spectre of boards would cast its shadow for the rest of our time in school. We entered class 8-D, Mr C. Innis, our class teacher. He also managed the scouts program in school.

It would be a momentous grade—some of us will be taught computer programming, the only ones in the country.

A New Me Every Class Year

Each class year ended with a 'Parent Teacher Meeting' (PTM); that's the day parents were called to collect report cards and discuss the conduct, character and progress of their sons. It was the most feared of all days in the year.

Depending on the interaction with teachers, we would come out smiling, solemn or tear-faced. Likewise, parents were beaming or scowling, averting everyone's gaze should they have been given reasons to be ashamed of their sons. Of course, the thick-skinned boys would be grinning as usual, knowing it was a biannual pattern with no new shocks. Their parents had the resigned look, their hopes for a brighter future for their sons resting on a miracle from whichever god they believed in.

Somehow, there was not much that was ever discussed about me; I was the guy who did no wrong, but I was also the guy with little to be excited about. Finishing in the top eight in a class of fifty was commendable enough, requiring no analysis or feedback.

The 'court appearance' over, it was time to mark a fresh beginning. By going to the stationery shop and picking up the pile of prescribed textbooks for the next higher class, notebooks and lots of brown paper. The ice cream cart did brisk business too on the day, most of us being treated to the fanciest item on the menu. No sooner were we home than we would get down to opening the packages and covering all books with brown paper. It was mandatory; there were regular checks and anyone with improper or torn covers would be reprimanded.

Despite knowing we will be tested more severely in the next higher grade; we looked forward to it with a sense of anticipation. It's as if we were starting a new life. We will be learning things for the first time. We will find ourselves in a higher orbit, a significant step-up from the previous year. There will be biological growth, and psychological evolution.

None of us went go through this alone; it happened to 250 of us simultaneously. We were exposed to the same influences and forces, but each of were shaped by them in our own unique mould. If only someone would have a shot a timelapse spread over thirteen years!

Unfortunately, the evolutionary graph follows a logarithmic pattern for most of us. The rise is sharp the first eighteen years, tapering off gradually to plateau off eventually. We get stuck in status-quo, committed to the same work and life pattern for decades of our adult life. We leave school behind, forgetting that life itself is one, if we allow ourselves to stay students. When we do, each year of our life can bring with it, the same sense of anticipation as a new class did. With it a fresh set of textbooks to teach something for the first time. With brown paper covering it.

The Only School Students to Be Taught Computer Programming
April 9, 1983

Surprise, surprise! The school modified their policy and computer programming would be taught as early as class eight. Fifty of the best were chosen across five sections and I made the cut too. Classes would take place on Saturdays. My excitement knew no bounds.

St. Columba's was the first school in the country to install computers to teach programming to its students. It would be a few years before others would emulate us. Most Indians had not seen a computer, did not even understand what one was. But Columbans would. The earliest machines were HCL, Eagle and Apple. Not all could be enrolled given the limited infrastructure, so those selected were automatically the elites. It came with a perk: air-conditioning; missing in the rest of the school and most Indian homes. We would jostle to access, not just the limited machine time, but also to stay cool.

We would be taught BASIC, a computer language. The first lesson was about two words: LOGIC and GIGO i.e., Garbage In, Garbage Out. What you put into the computer is what you get. All advancements in computing rely on these first principles. Because machines can never develop a mind like a human's. Those of us who grasped these concepts, excelled in the subject.

Br D'Souza would teach us—what a blessing that was. More so since he would leave school the following year. I would have missed out on being taught by one of the greatest teachers to have lived had this option not been given to us.

We Have the Computers. But Not a Text Book. So Write One!

St. Columba's may have been a pioneer in introducing computer studies at the school level and also been enterprising enough to raise funds to pay for the expensive machines. But there was a problem: there were no textbooks available to learn BASIC. Without it, the ISCE board would not recognise the subject.

Trust Br D'Souza to take it upon himself to write one. In double quick time. Students were enlisted to assist with the research, writing and editing. Wages took the form of pizzas at Nirula's, a coveted currency at the time. Just like that, the book *Chipping In* was out. Simple, graphical, lucid; even those who did not attend classes could teach themselves by reading this book. Because when you did, you could feel Br D'Souza himself was speaking to you.

Charlie Strikes. Those Who Flunk. And Those Who Score Ninety-Five.
April 15, 1983

Br D'Souza walked into class with results of mathematics in class seven finals. All those who scored below forty and above ninety-five were called out. Charlie was upset at the former for flunking and left a mark on their bottoms to show his annoyance. The other lot were gloating, expecting to be feted for their achievement. But Charlie did not spare them either—for making careless mistakes and missing out on scoring a hundred.

Rohit Valia, with a ninety-six, had been floating at the top of the world since results came out. He came down with a thud, landing on the backside left blue by Charlie.

James Hadley Chase? Seriously?
May – June 1983

Computer classes continued through the summer vacations and I booked every available hour programming away in the lab. There were days when Br D'Souza forced me to go home, lest my mother wonder where I was. Remember, we could not take telephony for granted back then.

There was another incentive to go to school during the vacations: an exception was made and we were allowed to borrow all the books we could consume from the library. It was no different from the proverbial pot of gold for us. Yes, it was also an era when all of us read books. While others picked the classics, PG Wodehouses, Agatha Christies and other Perry Masons, I spent the summers reading James Hadley Chase.

Br D'Souza raised his eyebrows when issuing me the books, asking if I was sure I wanted to read these. I said yes. He signed off, offering no further opinion.

India Wins the Cricket World Cup: The Old Order Changeth

It is one of those moments when everyone remembers where they were. I was in Ambala with the extended family to attend the wedding of a cousin. All ceremonies were put on hold to watch India upset the West Indies in the finals to lift the Prudential Cup and be crowned cricket's new world champions.

Having won the previous two editions, the West Indies were the overwhelming favourites, their team considered invincible. They were cruising in the modest chase of 183 when Kapil Dev ran for his life to catch the ball that sent superstar Viv Richards back to the pavilion. A batting collapse followed; the 'rag-tag' bunch had done the unimaginable!

The other memory etched in everyone's minds is Kapil Dev's match-winning knock of 175 against Zimbabwe in a group match, coming in when India was down five wickets for just seventeen runs. Strangely, no one outside the stadium has ever seen that epic innings: the match was not telecast and recording lost.

India's victory was a watershed in world cricket. The mighty West Indies went into a decline and are yet to be feared by any opposition like they were back then. More importantly, there was a political shift: centre of power moved from England to India in the coming decades. The Indian board would go on to amass wealth most other administrative bodies even in the developed world cannot aspire for—not just cricket but across all sports. With money came might, India assuming top positions in the International Cricket Council, dictating terms to suit its interests. The Indian Premier League launched in the 21st century would add to its coffers. With every cricketer around the world seeking to play for one of the teams, the international playing calendar is now designed around the IPL.

The old order changeth, the excesses of the new not necessarily appealing to every fan's taste.

The Four of Us: BFFs (Until School at Least)

Anish Tawakley and I got into a scuffle. He was stronger and getting the better of me when I managed a manoeuvre and ended up sitting on him. He started protesting about it being an unfair tactic in a fight, breathless under my weight, but I was just playing to my strength like he was. Manav Abrol was watching all through, amused to bits. The stalemate might not have broken had Anish's mother not come out and separated us. We were fighting just outside his house and Manav finally had to alert her.

All three had moved into the same neighbourhood in Hauz Khas. Anish and I had been together in section D but barely interacted; Manav was in section B and a relative stranger to me until we met in the same bus. After a rocky start, Anish and I became best friends.

Within a short time, along with Jayant Tripathi from section D, we became four. Always hanging out together, in school and outside. Jayant lived in Shahjahan Road so he interacted lesser; in any case, he was more into reading. I moved out from Hauz Khas after a year, but stayed in Sheikh Sarai and Asian Games Village for the next eight years. The proximity ensured the three of us met regularly even when in college. We went our separate ways after this, meeting each other one-on-one but overdue all four together.

Before I got socially close to this group, I hung around with my namesake Ajay Khanna in school. I reconnected with him in our late thirties in London; that's where he shared his hurt at being ignored after I became pally with Anish way back in seventh grade. He had been nursing the wound for decades.

Call Me Jumbo

July 9, 1983

Br D'Souza started addressing me with a moniker: Jumbo. He did not use my real name after that and he had no qualms addressing me as Jumbo irrespective who else was present.

I checked myself out in the mirror many times—I considered myself the best-looking guy in the class. And certainly not overweight. Maybe I was being called Jumbo out of fondness and not as a form of body teasing. Many years later, when I would be a trimmer version of myself, I tried a few of my old clothes. They hung on me like sacks. Maybe I was Jumbo!

Teachers Are Not a He or She

August 8, 1983

'Teachers are not a "he" or a "she". They are Sir, Ma'am, Mr Thomas, Mrs Singh.'

I don't know where this came from, but Miss Khosla told the class sternly. Elders and seniors deserve our respect, and we cannot address them as a he or a she. To illustrate her point: 'Mrs Wintle is coming', not 'she is coming'. Likewise, 'Mr Landale is playing football', not 'he is playing football.'

To date, I cannot get myself to refer to anyone older or senior as a he or she in my spoken words. Strange how some lessons, even when delivered in passing, just stay with you.

Unquotable Quotes

Some words become legendary. There was no exception in our school. I compiled a sample. Some can be attributed, some cannot. Even when they can be, one cannot be fully sure. But they float in ether; it is up to you and Ripley to believe it or not. Hindi words and slangs have deliberately not been translated.

'If you can't do, you are a *Gan-doo!*' – Mr Pacheco, challenging the class with a physics problem on the blackboard.

'Boys, the weekend is coming. Go make your ends weak.' – Mr Pacheco

'Open the window and let the climate come in.' – Repeated by many teachers, when classrooms would get stuffy.

'Bloodif!': This is how most of us were addressed by the ever-impatient P.T. teacher, Mr Sharma.

'Bete': That's how Mr Verma called most students, in a style unique to him. *Bete* means son.

'I will curse you and God will punish you!': Mrs Thomas when the class got too noisy.

Funny Only if You Understand Hindi

'Hanso ge toh phanso ge' (If you laugh, you will be trapped) – Mrs Khera, Hindi teacher warning students if any were caught laughing in class.

'Aur Lehna Singh ne kaha ... Mukul aap class se get out ho jao' (Lehna Singh, a character in one of our textbooks, said Mukul Dev Kaushal may get out of the class): Mrs Khera

Student: 'Teri gand me chipkali' (Hope you have a lizard in your ass)

Brother Farrel (who did not know Hindi): 'Yes, I know the ground is very slippery.'

Jogaisms

Mr Joginder Singh, popularly known as Joga, Mechanical Drawing teacher and football coach was famous for his quips. Not all such utterances have witnesses, but everyone swears they were truly attributable to him:

'The principal just passed away.': When spotting the principal walk by in the corridor while classes were on.

'Br. D'Souza is rotating in the corridors.'

'All the playboys come to the field.': Calling the football team for practice.

'You can get them quickly. Your home is only a five-minute walk by cycle.': When Vikram had forgotten to bring his football shoes.

'Meet me behind the class when I am empty.'

'Both of you three come and meet me at the back of the period.'

'Mr Chadha, there is very low air in your previous tyre.': Alerting Mr Chadha to the low pressure in the rear tyre of his scooter.

Summoning 'Mullah Pappoos' Over Public Address System

August 16, 1983

'Would Mullah from class 7-B come down to the office?'

All classrooms had a speaker connected to the headmaster's office. A crackling sound, a hiss usually preceded any announcement, as if to get us into an attentive mode. So when 'Mullah' was summoned over the PA system, everyone in the Middle School wondered who would have such a name.

Turns out it was Aditya Mubayi, another of Br D'Souza's monikers, derived from the former's Kashmiri ethnicity. I suppose Brother did this with those he was fond of; Aditya was the prodigy in quizzing, earning many a laurel for the school. Not amused with the 'publicity' he got, he stomped to the headmaster's office, seething with embarrassment, demanding an explanation.

'At least I did not add the other part of your name, Pappoos,' said Br D'Souza.

'Thank you so much sir, you just made my day. Thank you for small mercies,' was all that a red-faced Aditya could say.

To date, Aditya does not know what 'Pappoos' is.

Drawing 'Tadpoles' in the Textbook
August 24, 1983

Mukul Dev Kaushal was drawing penises in the *Radiant Reader* workbook and the English teacher, Miss Khosla, caught him doing it.

'Why are you defacing the book, drawing tadpoles on the pages,' she enquired. Mukul had to keep his lips tightly pressed; had he so much as parted them to speak, he would have fallen off his chair laughing. Miss Khosla just whacked the book on his head and moved on.

A Wallet for Mr Innis
September 5, 1983

Badal Gulati, Ashish Sarna, Sunil Kochhar and I pooled in to buy our class teacher, Mr Innis, a wallet for Teacher's Day. I was entrusted to pick one from the market.

It was a day free of lectures, each class deciding its own entertainment. Ours rented a television set and VCR to screen a film. We were playing *An Officer and a Gentleman* when Mr Innis walked in during a kissing scene; he immediately turned it off. Fortunately, someone had thought of a Plan B and we switched to *E.T. the Extra-Terrestrial*.

It was also a chaotic day and we were not able to find a window for the four of us to present the wallet to Mr Innis. I finally found him sitting free but others were not around, so I anyway went up and presented it to him. I mumbled the names of the other three too; he thanked me and that's it.

When the others suggested we give it, I said I already have. They were clearly pissed, despite my assurances that I mentioned all the names. They (rightly) complained it does not make the same impression as going up in person. I don't know if they ever held a grudge and, if so, for how long.

Slap Yourself!
September 14, 1983

Charlie was having a bad day when eight juicy prospects walked in. Finally, some action! Just when Br D'Souza took Charlie in his right hand, one of them, Rohit Kaushik, fainted. All of them were ordered to get out; it turned out to be a good day for them, but a worse one for Charlie! Rohit should have been treated to a king's feast by others for his 'act.'

The eight must have really upset the Hindi teacher, Mrs Karandikar, to have been sent off to the headmaster's office. Her standard punishment was, 'Slap yourself!'

Yes, you had to slap your own self in full view of the class. And keep at it till the teacher wasn't satisfied you had hit yourself hard enough.

But did you know who had the toughest time of all? Nirbhay, her son. He was in her class, his conduct always under scrutiny. He felt ostracized because others thought he had access to the question paper. If he had any advantage, he would have done better than scoring 60 per cent in class ten.

The 'slap yourself' was standard punishment at home too!

Snatching Captaincy from Best Friend
October 8, 1983

Mr Lockwood appointed Rajesh Bharadwaj the captain of the class cricket team, granting him the authority to select the players.

Trials were scheduled on a Saturday morning at the Talkatora Gardens. It seems the whole class landed up. Rajesh spread everyone far and wide to field—giving only a few the opportunity to show their mettle with the bat or the ball. I bowled one over, maintained a straight line, gave no runs away and knocked Savio's bails off the last ball.

Yet I was not selected. I was disappointed. But Rohit Srivastava was miffed. He was not asked to bowl or bat, so how could he make the cut? Seems Rajesh had already decided the eleven he wanted, the trials a farce. Weren't Rajesh and Rohit close friends? 'I will show the BKL (expletive!),' muttered Rohit.

Rohit signed up at the cricket academy run by Gurcharan Singh, a coach of the national team. He did not miss any sessions for months and it showed in his game. He not only took away captaincy from Rajesh for himself the following year, but also made it to the school team.

The (Law of the) Jungle at the Back of the School Bus

St. Columba's had its own versions of class divide. What else do you expect when you pack in 3,000 boys within a campus? We did not descend to the darkness we studied in *Lord of the Flies*, but we were no less territorial than the characters in the book.

Nowhere was it more pronounced than in the school bus, particularly during the afternoon drive back. The more senior a class you were in, the stronger your claim to standing room at the back of the bus and on the footboards. As my good friend Sachin Kukreja put it aptly in the school magazine:

'Evil for good' is the law of the jungle. It is also the law of an even wilder place—the back of the Z bus of St. Columba's. With activities like tie-snapping, bird-watching, teacher baiting, bullying, not to mention on-the-spot quiz and histrionic contests, tests of skill and daring on the footboard and aggrieved accounts of what happened that day—it is more dramatic than you can imagine it to be. Adding to unexpected nature of this place are

the frequent clashes between the oppressed junior classes (literally speaking) and the brutal land owning or rather back of the bus owning seniors, resulting inevitably in a brutal ejection of the former from the latter's domain.

I would emphasise on the noble art of tie-snapping, a remarkable exercise in ingenuity. This thin strip of green and yellow striped cloth becomes, in the inventive hands of a Columban, a whip, a lasso, a rope, or a highly effective strangulating device. Once the cheery functions of such weapons, such as committing semi-homicides, are over, the tie at once becomes transformed into 'medical supplies' for the injured, bandages, tourniquets and such like.

Another fascinating game boys play, rivalled in effort only by tiffin grabbing is Who-Shouts-Louder. A very fruitful interchange takes place, and radical and important ideas on highly relevant issues of today like, who flicked whose chemistry practicals copy, or which teacher did what are aired, which could not but fail to elevate, edify and inspire us.

I fantasize about the tantalising things I could indulge in, if only I had the guts to march upto the seniors and say, 'Look, I've paid my fees too, I have a right to be there.' Such comments however are reserved discreetly for my comrades, with whom I plan ambitious raids in the not too distant future.

And oh, those seniors! When they were juniors I bet they were picked on by their seniors - so why must they do the same thing to us. Just wait. When I become a senior, I'll ...

A Columban Plays Modernite in Shekhar Kapur's *Masoom*
October 24, 1983

Rajan Shahi, of class 4-B, found his two minutes of fame via Bollywood.

He played the role of Saeed Jaffrey's son in the movie, *Masoom,* based on the Hollywood hit, *Man, Woman and Child.* A directorial debut by Shekhar Kapur, legendary star Dev Anand's nephew, it would go on to win many awards of the day. Rajan had only a limited role, that of a spoilt brat studying in Modern School. The director captured it very well; families like those depicted in the movie were more likely to send their children—boys and girls—to Modern School than to a missionary school. Rajan captured the body language of such kids perfectly.

While the movie was being shot, I got a chance to be on set for a day—and witnessed the moment when lead star Naseeruddin Shah brings his illegitimate son home.

Appealing to Softer Side to Get Test Cancelled
November 1, 1983

You did not want to upset Mrs Rebello, not that it took much to rile up the biology teacher.

Our class got under her skin with the pandemonium we created. We would not quieten down no matter how much she screamed at us. Then she delivered a blow to finally stun us into silence. There would be an unscheduled test the following day, and we were given an insane number of chapters to prepare. Before we could protest or plead mercy, she walked away.

No matter how hard I tried, I could not get my head around the texts. Biology was the subject I hated most. Then I did something unimaginable: I called the teacher home, apologised on behalf of the class and requested her to call off the test. Surprise, surprise! A softer side of her gave in.

I called up the few classmates whose numbers I had to deliver the good news. Word spread, but not all got the message. They burnt the midnight oil to prepare, only to find the rest of gloating at their misery.

Side note: In class one, I would sometimes miss my bus Z13 at Pandara Road. My parents walked me down a few hundred yards where another bus Z2 stopped. We were not allowed to travel in buses other than ours, but exceptions were sometimes made. Mrs Rebello travelled in Z2 and would scold me loudly for being indisciplined. I would stand still till she quietened down and then take a seat next to Rohit Valia. I had dreaded the day she would teach me biology.

Racing Champion for a Lap—Before Running Out of Steam
November 11, 1983

I was desperate to make a mark in any sport and considered athletics on the annual Sports Day. Since no one else did from our section, I signed up for the 800 metres race to be run over four laps of the Middle School grounds.

I just showed up on the day —with no practice. 'Did not seem such a big deal,' I thought. The whistle blew—there was no gun—and we are off. I sprinted ahead—leaving the rest of the pack far behind. 'Why were they jogging, and not running?' I did not care; the crowd was cheering me on to maintain the lead.

The first lap went fine but something seemed wrong after that. I was feeling the human equivalent of a sputtering engine, with a side stitch building in intensity. I was out of breath, holding my abdomen tight. My race was over in less than 300 metres.

I felt ridiculous. Everyone must be thinking of me to be a clown for not pacing myself. I would never run a race again.

I was finally awarded a certificate in sports—our class 8-D finished runners-up in basketball. It was a silly contest actually—none of the teams knew how to play, and the referees had a hard time enforcing rules. This was my only podium finish in thirteen years.

Mens sana in corpore sano: Healthy Mind in a Healthy Body

If someone mistook St. Columba's to be a sports school, they would not be too far from the truth. Because there was a time when you would always find boys playing for as long as there was light.

When the Provincial of the Christian Brothers was planning on building a school, it is believed, he went looking for a suitable playing field. Only after earmarking a space for the purpose, he allocated the remaining area to school buildings. Sports and physical training were a vital part of the curriculum, resonating the spirit of *'Mens sana in corpore sano'* or 'healthy mind in a healthy body.' Over the years, as budgets permitted, a swimming pool, a tennis court and a multi-purpose indoor gymnasium have been added.

From middle school onwards, inter-section matches have been the norm for each class. These were fierce contests, classmates cheering with patriotic fervour. Since most of us stayed in the same section throughout, performance of our respective teams granted us bragging rights and created a 'class' system of its own!

The annual Sports Day established itself as a red-letter day on the school calendar. For a month leading up to it, the regular, boring P.T. classes took on a new importance and urgency. Students were endlessly put through their paces practicing their various drills—Swedish, Club, Dumbbell, Maze with the pièce de résistance being the spectacular Gymnastic display. The inter-class march-past competition trophy was probably the most coveted of all, with many a 'free' period spent practicing with the monotonous drone 'left, right, left … ' ringing out across the field and easily heard by those in the classrooms. Boys stayed back to prepare for athletics events, building their stamina and pace, praying they did not get injured.

As the school expanded, the Sports Day moved from the school field to either the National Stadium or the Shivaji Stadium, depending on their availability. It allowed the spectacle to look even grander, with stands filled with parents and siblings. Flags fluttering in the wind, starter guns firing, whistles blowing, loudpeakers blaring, music playing, medals being awarded by guests of honour—for our athletes, the St. Columba's Sports Day mattered more than the Olympics!

Of course, like everything else, things change. A sense of calm seems to have descended on the school's sports facilities, with voluntary participation at a low. As former headmaster Br Fernandes summed it: 'There has been a rebalance in importance afforded to outdoor activities and the classroom. Years ago, games and sports were vigorously encouraged by the Brothers, teachers and more importantly, parents. More time, of course, was available for these activities which were unhindered by social media, electronic gadgets and above all private tuitions—the bane of today's educational system.'

Remorse? Burgers From Br D'Souza After Caning
November 25, 1983

DJ Singh should have saved the ice-cream for a cold pack after his encounter with Charlie.

He was licking a lolly in the class queue, assuming no one would notice. Until Br D'Souza called him. Oops! DJ threw the evidence into the hedges, but it was too late. He was told to stretch his hands, getting one on the right palm, then the left and then the right again. He did not flinch for even a moment before being told to get out. Only when out of sight did he rub his hands in pain since he had not wanted the headmaster to know.

DJ complained to his father, who showed up in the school the following day. One does not know what transpired in the meeting, but Br D'Souza issued DJ a few handwritten coupons—called parchis—for burgers in the canteen, an olive leaf of sorts. Not a bad trade!

Parents Were Not Told When We Got Caned. Lest We Get Whacked at Home Too!

So here's the thing: it was the rarest of rare exceptions when someone whined at home that they suffered from corporal punishment in school. Why make our humiliation public? Parents had a tendency to ignore the incident anyway. If they did land up in school to take the matter up with the concerned teacher, it would make their son come across as a sissy.

The biggest reason for not telling them? 'You must have done something wrong to provoke the reaction from your teacher,' is what we were likely to hear from them. Followed by a dressing down or even additional whacks. There would be no trial, no opportunity to defend ourselves.

Gifting Winner Certificates to Friends
December 5, 1983

Why is Varun Pawha getting a certificate when he never took the field?

We had won the inter-class cricket tournament, a big surprise considering other sections had bigger stars than ours. I had witnessed all the games and Varun was not even spotted sitting amongst the reserves.

Turns out Varun was keen to get a certificate in any sport and his best friend and team captain, Rajesh Bharadwaj, obliged. He agreed to include his name if he promised not to insist on playing. That was acceptable, considering Varun did not know one side of the bat from the other.

I wanted to cry foul; I was a better cricketer than him but was not picked. But I let it be, joining the victory celebrations instead.

Br D'Souza's Talents Include Playing Waiter
December 17, 1983

No one can keep track of Br D'Souza's talents, with new ones emerging at a frequent clip. The latest revelation was his ability to play waiter.

He was attending the Master's dinner at the five-star Claridges hotel when some ladies mistook him to be one of the butlers—because of his 'shoddy' cassock. One of them beckoned to be served; instead of taking offence, he picked a tray to serve them hors d'oeuvres. Profuse apologies followed when the lady realized who he was!

The state of his cassock caught everyone's attention. When asked why he could not get one in better condition, he would say he is waiting for a Brother of his size to die to inherit his.

There was more to his attire. If you ever pointed out to two different socks on his feet—not infrequent—he would look down, feign a pensive look, and then reply, 'You know what, I have another pair exactly like this in my wardrobe!'

Mr Massey Cross for 'Noughty' Behaviour
January 9,1984

What's worse than being caned? Being caned in biting cold. That's why Gaurav Mehra went 'OUCH, OUCH, OUCH, OUCH, OUCH, ouch!' That's five strong whacks, and one soft.

Mr Massey caught him playing Noughts and Crosses with Pankaj Baijal during class—an offence—attracting maximum punishment. While Pankaj accepted his fate quietly, Gaurav made a show of it with his utterances. He was nearly in tears, and so were the rest of us—with laughter.

Dismissed as Monitor Twice on the Same Day
January 17, 1984

The class just refused to settle down and Mr Innis reminded me of my job to maintain order as the class monitor while he checked test papers. 'But they are not listening to me,' I submitted. 'If you are in the right, learn to take a stand in life,' he retorted. 'I am dismissing you as monitor,' he added without a pause. I humbly went back to my seat.

In fifteen minutes, he called me back to tell me he is removing me as monitor since I had no control over the class. 'But you already fired me a few minutes back,' I replied cheekily. The scowl on his face developed deeper ridges, his fingers rubbing the forehead to comfort his migraine.

Within a few months, I would be appointed as one of the school prefects despite a 'tarnished' record as class monitor.

Losing Your Lunch Money to the Gods
January 28, 1984

You don't mess with the Gods. Nor play pranks. They have no sense of humour.

Mohit Varma, KVK Vikram and I had taken DTC bus 540—they for sports, me for a computer class. We got dropped off at the All-India Radio headquarters, a ten-minute walk from school. Being a Saturday, we could see lamps on the pavements for Shani Dev, the Saturn God. Made of iron, with a two-dimensional cut-out of the God sticking out from its edge, these lamps have burning wicks dipped in mustard oil. It's a ritual, and a business model, since time immemorial—they appear magically on Saturday mornings on streets, believers dropping coins in the oil. The lamps disappear by sunset just as mysteriously.

Mohit decided to play the fool, tearing his bus ticket into half as offering—only to look aghast at a Rs 10 note in his hand which he had inadvertently ripped into two. That was his meal ticket at Nirula's later in the day! We looked at the cut-out of Shani Dev with moist eyes: his with regret, ours with amusement.

Vikram and he would still go, sharing a burger between them, paid for by Vikram's intact Rs 10 note. Mohit never looked the Saturn God in the eye again.

I Programmed Book Cricket on a Computer. Br D'Souza Loved It.
February 7, 1984

Br D'Souza was hooked to the game of 'Book Cricket' I had programmed. I was his 'Man of the Match' without taking the field. But I almost got into big trouble for plagiarism.

Venkatraman Krishnaswamy was going around complaining that I had stolen his program. When summoned for an explanation, I was in a spot. Lie or tell the truth? To my good fortune, I decided to come clean. I admitted to overhearing Venkat voicing the idea of making the game, but the entire programming was mine. No action was taken—and I was awarded top honours in the subject. In any case, I coded the game weeks after he had spoken about it—he did not intend padding up for the game anyway, so my conduct could not be described unsportsmanlike.

For the uninitiated: Book Cricket is a game boys play to beat boredom in class. We drafted fantasy teams to play against each other. We turn pages randomly of any reasonably thick book—and check the last digit of the left-hand page number. Two, four and six are the number of runs by a batsman, while a zero or eight meant 'out.' I did so very often—my notebooks were full of scoresheets. I simulated the same on the computer—players could make their teams and numbers would pop up randomly. Br D'Souza took it like a boy himself, spending hours playing.

Tempting Charlie

It seemed Br Pinto and Br D'Souza had an arsenal of canes in their offices, each designed to serve a different purpose. They, the canes I mean, were certain to be twitching to twang, so it was best not to tempt them. And yet, some boys could not resist doing so.

Rahul Dev Arora certainly sought Charlie out. It was a drug to him. He got whacked once for signing his diary himself—teachers had an uncanny ability to spot forged signatures of our parents. He was caught twice for bunking school and paid for it. Br Pinto spotted him smoking in the school bus; the source of fumes shifted from his mouth to his backside after Charlie was done with it.

Competing with Rahul for maximum guilty verdicts was Mukul Dev Kaushal. Whatever any of us did, it was a subset of what Mukul had done. In other words, he had committed every possible crime in the school. Including, but not limited to, bunking, cocky behaviour, flunking subjects, masturbating, pranks and general misbehaviour. Whenever there was the equivalent of a police lineup of suspects, Mukul would always be called in.

Worst was catching Charlie's attention for absolutely avoidable misdemeanours. We were advised not to be seen in corridors without reason. If shoes were dirty, we knew we had to find a silk cotton flower and shine them up with its nectar. Ensure the tie was knotted properly, the belt tightened and shirt tucked in. Br D'Souza would randomly call any of us out, scan us head to toe, count the number of infringements and give us two swings of Charlie for each.

Golden advice: No matter what, if you were caught, speak the truth. That was your only hope, even if feeble, of being spared.

Farewell Dance in a Skirt by a Sikh 'Gypsy'
February 22, 1984

The guy in a shawl and dark glasses got away. The one dancing in a skirt did not.

Everyone wanted to know about the 'surd' (Sikh) adorned in a skirt, blouse, ghungroos (ankle bells) and beads dancing to an audience of fifty before the principal, Br Pinto, broke the party. Sukhdeep Chattwal was given marching orders to the principal's office. The bells jingled as he walked the corridors; half the Senior School paused what they were doing to look at him. The rouge on his cheeks turned a deep pink with embarrassment.

What emboldened him to put on such a show? Two days back, a classmate walked around draped in a shawl, sporting dark glasses. Six more did the same the following day. What the heck? Their batch was on the verge of graduating from

St. Columba's School, so Sukhdeep decided to raise the style bar. And thus, the gypsy act.

Br Pinto was not amused. Sukhdeep was suspended for the remaining week, as was the rest of the class. 'Why the others?' he protested.

'For enjoying the performance.'

Thirteen years in school ended in suspension for the class. Sukhdeep, of course, was given a rousing welcome by the class waiting outside the gates. He would be their hero(ine) for life!

The Final Massacre by Br D'Souza
February 24, 1984

Br D'Souza's Charlie would go out swinging. Smeared with the 'blood' of fourteen boys.

Noticing a higher than usual level of absentees in the ninth grade, Br D'Souza picked the phone to call those missing. In most cases, the mothers of boys picked up. Pretending to be their friend, he got each of the boys on the line. Changing the tone back to his own, he told them who he was and ordered them to show up in school within half an hour or they would not be allowed in for a month—hence missing their final exams and promotion to tenth.

We could only speculate how those boys got into uniform and scampered to report within the deadline given. If they were expecting any leniency, then they were daydreaming. None would be able to sit comfortably for days after the benders they received. The pain would be mitigated eventually but the trauma would linger.

Br D'Souza would leave school soon after. The fourteen made for the perfect farewell party for Charlie.

Why Did I Never Meet Br D'Souza Again?

I identify myself as a traveller. I was one, literally, when I worked as a travel writer for fifteen years and metaphorically all my life. Yet I procrastinated meeting Br D'Souza—despite a deep desire to. I even travelled to Guwahati a few times; I could so easily have met him, his home, Shillong, just a short drive away. Yet I did not.

I assumed there was all the time in the world to. But there wasn't. Because he passed before I could pay him a visit. Sand always passes through the hourglass of life.

It will remain one of the biggest regrets of my life. I have no one to blame but myself. Agonizing over it won't take me back in time, but I have learnt to cherish the present, live in the moment, do what is important now. That's when we can look at the past fondly and assure ourselves a future of hope and fulfilment.

Wasn't this what Br D'Souza's life was all about? Living.

On a lighter note: Whenever I would think of meeting Br D'Souza, I would have wanted to test if he remembered calling me Jumbo. I would not have been surprised if he had greeted me with that moniker the moment he saw me.

Awarded Excellent in Computer Studies
February 29, 1984

We called ourselves programmers hereon. Some excellent at it, like me.

The class of fifty were handed out their certificates. Kanchan Mitra and Saeed-Ul Islam came out top, with theirs marked 'Brilliant.' Along with two others, I got the next best 'Excellent.' The rest were 'Very Good' or 'Good.'

I was thrilled with my ranking. It also showed I had been absolved of any unethical behaviour in the book cricket program episode.

Logically, I should have made a career in information technology. My brain is wired to comprehend how programs flow; I could have been 'excellent' at coding too. Anyone who could, was picking this stream for higher studies. Not able to belong to a pack, I went off in a different direction. There were struggles in the choices I made but I gathered and lived more stories along the way than many others who took the secure road to material riches.

Ranked Second in Class. But No Awards for Me.
March 30, 1984

The class eight results were out ... and I finished second. My highest rank ever. I had been jostling between fifth and eighth in a class of fifty all these years.

The top two in class receive a memento and a mention in the school magazine. I would always resent those who received it in the past. I was going to hold one of my own finally.

Then came a double blow. The school discontinued the practice of awarding the mementoes. There was a logic to the decision, but my brain was too fuzzed to understand it. To make it worse, my name was missing in the magazine.

I was tied for second position with Dinesh Sehgal—he got mentioned but not me. I felt in the dumps.

Who could I complain to? The unfairness of it!

Entered Class Nine: The Bridge Years to Adulthood

April 3, 1984

You can call the ninth and tenth as the bridge years between childhood and the real world, when we would no longer be cloistered in a sanctuary called St. Columba's. The two grades are also hyphenated because the ICSE boards included the curriculum of both—a dreaded proposition, keeping us on our toes for two years.

These would be years of evolution in each of us, biological and psychological. The way we talk, the way we walk, the way we think would change. While some would hold onto their juvenility for their dear life, others would be expected to mature, to gradually unveil who we would become. In our physical beings and in personal and professional choices we would go on to make. Because decisions taken in these, and the following years, could well determine the lives we would lead.

Br D'Souza was in line to be the class teacher of 9-D but he made a sudden decision to move to the Northeast. Br F.M. Fernandes would take his place in our section, and become the new headmaster of Middle School.

Br Fernandes, an alumnus of the school, was gracious enough to admit he was taking over from Br D'Souza, who he called a creative and innovative genius, and by no stretch of imagination would he be able to fill his shoes. Furthermore, he disliked administration, and managing over 1500 students and seventy teachers in the Middle School was a daunting task for him. He would also be supervising some of his own teachers when he was a student here. Being required to teach would compensate for it though, making his days rewarding and fulfilling.

Then there was the matter of a new student joining our batch this year: Rahul Gandhi. In section A. We expected him to be in our section D though since the headmaster was our class teacher. His sister, Priyanka, enrolled in neighbouring CJM. The two would keep their respective school administrations in a state of heightened alertness. Not for long though, for tragic reasons.

I Am a School Prefect

April 9, 1984

The list of school prefects came out. Five were picked from each section, for a total of twenty-five. I was not surprised to be one of them, but I couldn't understand why Mahijit Singh and Yajuvendra Anand were picked? They were the troublemakers, their grades not ones to be flaunted when uncles and aunts came calling at home. Maybe their tall, muscular builds would be useful to manage mobs? Perhaps a psychological experiment: tame the unruly by burdening them with responsibilities. Like bouncers in a night club, fierce guys forced to be at their best behaviour.

We were each presented a badge saying PREFECT with the school emblem—pinned to our ties or blazers for a year. The honour was more smoke than fire though; we did not have much to do, nor did we enjoy any powers. We were like a reserve force—trained and equipped, to be called up in an emergency. In a peculiar miss, the group photograph of prefects that year did not feature in the school mag.

Learning Photography with Rahul Gandhi

We were given a choice. Sign up for photography classes or enlist in the SUPW program, Socially Useful Productive Work. I chose the former.

On day one, we were asked to either get a film camera of our own or buy one through our tutor, Mr Jacob. I paid Rs 500 for an Agfa model. We had regular sessions after that but I have no recollection of being explained even the basics of photography. I felt scammed.

Rahul Gandhi was in our class too; I tried to strike up conversations with him, but he was too reserved. If nothing else, we could have made the course worth it with a photo together.

Would SUPW have been more rewarding? Maybe. What did one do under that? Participate in first aid training by the Red Cross. Assist students struggling with their course work so they may do better in exams. There was a non-profit called Life Society in Dakshinpuri who ran a school for the marginalised; we provided their students with time, medicine, clothes and even entertainment. Flea markets were organized to sell used clothes and shoes, the collection further funding causes. Students also lent a hand and arranged resources for other organizations like the Cheshire Home and those running dispensaries and creches for the poor.

How to Tame Shahrukh Khan's Unruly Class
April 16, 1984

Shahrukh Khan's class 12-C had become too unruly and Br Pinto had to call upon lieutenants who could be relied upon to enforce discipline.

A new maths teacher, brother of another middle school teacher Mrs Popli, had moved from Kenya and joined the school a year earlier. He was a mis-hire, his command of the subject not adequate for a bright class like 12-C. They saw through his limitations and gave him hell for it. They may have been enjoying the thrills of creating the ruckus, but did not realize they were losing out on the education with such distractions.

The school had to let go of the teacher but there was both the need of a tutor and a disciplinarian. Br Pinto thus requested Mr Pokhriyal to take charge and he gladly took up the challenge.

A diffident personality when he joined, Mr Pokhriyal learnt to wield the power of Charlie within a couple of years. With an uncanny ability to remember names of each of his students, he would catch them off guard by calling out their name with a question—while looking at another student. If daydreaming, or looking out of the window wistfully, or reading the latest edition of *Mastram* when your name was called was a surefire way to land you in trouble. Digging into our tiffin boxes when a teacher's back was towards us was common through the school; Mr Pokhriyal learnt to quickly turn around, spot a boy with his mouth full and give him a tight one on his cheek. Good luck to the food not flying out or choking you. Such tactics instilled the fear of God and Mr Pokhriyal in the class, and it did not take long for them to sober up.

Mr Pokhriyal had a very good voice, a jukebox you don't need to put coins in, for him to get started. 'I may be a singer, but students should know there can be a rude and cruel side to me when required,' Mr Pokhriyal would say. With Br Pinto firmly supportive of his methods, order was brought to 12-C in the final year of Shahrukh Khan.

Who Prepares for University Entrance Exams Four Years in Advance?
April 30, 1984

Anish Tawakley is nuts. He had subscribed to the foundation course by Brilliant Tutorials to prepare for the entrance exam to Indian Institute of Technology or IIT. Four years in advance!

No doubt admission to one of the five IITs was almost a sure-shot passport to the best of career opportunities; only 2000 in the country made the cut. Additional coaching was a must since the school curriculum did not prepare you adequately for the advanced test. Most aspirants around the country signed up for correspondence courses, Brilliant and Agarwal Classes being the most popular at the time. They sent study material and self-assessment tests by posts, holding in-person sessions periodically.

The trend was to get down to preparing for the exam in class eleven; starting earlier may not give you significant advantage and you risked burnout. To each their own though. Manav, Jayant and I would only roll our eyes and let Anish be.

Anish did make it to IIT, pursuing Mechanical Engineering at their Delhi campus. He has gone on to make a successful corporate career but continued to stay as nerdy at work as he was in school. Manav, Jayant, and I have stayed cool lifelong.

When 99 Per cent is Not Good Enough
May 12, 1984

'You are a good friend, why don't you urge him to work harder? Ninety-nine is good, but how could he lose that one mark?'

Rajesh Bharadwaj did not know where to look while Dinesh Sehgal's mother was fretting. He had gone across to Dinesh's house casually, but he had not expected to find a mother hyperventilating. He kept nodding his head, mumbling that he will talk to his friend, praying she does not ask the question he was dreading. But she did.

'How much did you score?'

'Fifty-seven, auntie. You can take one mark off me and give to Dinesh. There is not much difference between fifty-seven and fifty-six but there is a wide gap between ninety-nine and hundred.'

Dinesh and I had tied for the second position in class eight and I, too, was pressured to do well. But I might have run away from home had my father stretched his expectations to such extremes. Dinesh's rank fell dramatically in the coming years, possibly buckling under the weight of parental expectations.

Juhi Chawla: The Country's Sweetheart
July 9, 1984

The country stayed awake late into the night—for the first ever live telecast of the Miss Universe pageant. From Miami, USA.

Everyone was rooting for Miss India—Juhi Chawla—who would go on to make a stellar career in Bollywood and be the 'sweetest one' long before Cameron Diaz claimed the phrase as her own. The crown went to Yvonne Ryding of Sweden but not before Juhi won the national costume round. Of course, all we spoke about in the school the following day was about the swimsuit round. A celebrity from India had never been seen in skimpy clothing on live television before.

I watched the event on a black and white television set in my grandmother's house. It was a wonder no power cuts interrupted the show, nor did anyone have to go to the roof to adjust the antenna to compensate for poor reception. The authorities deserved to be crowned for such exceptional service, a rare occurrence.

Kung-Fu with the Headmaster
July 17, 1984

If Badal was auditioning for the role of Cheshire Cat, he would have got it on the day he got into a kung-fu duel with the headmaster.

He had the audacity to be walking the corridors without a tie, the shirt hanging out. When confronted about his attire, he didn't say a word, grinning and even snickering when the question was repeated. That's when Br Fernandes lost his cool, striking Badal with his hands. After the first few blows, Badal upped his defences, moving his arms kung-fu style to block the strikes. Passers-by stopped to see 'Jackie Chang' entertainment which money cannot buy.

Badal did not lose his Cheshire Cat grin for even a moment. He entered the class with the swagger of a Bollywood star and was received as one!

Cockroaches Down Their Shirts
July 25, 1984

The cockroaches sacrificed their lives for science ... and for the entertainment of juveniles.

Biology—the subject I cringed about most in school—required us to dissect cockroaches, the first time I would be handling a lifeless body. The thought of it is abhorrent now but not then. How else could I get myself to pocket some cockroaches (yikes!) after the lab session, along with Sachin Kukreja?

Where were we taking them? Not to accord the martyrs a state funeral. But to slide down the shirts of others in the school bus. We laughed like idiots when we did—but deep within, neither of us was amused. We pretended to be. Kushraj Wadhwa, the "man" amongst us, only muttered to us: 'Grow up!'

I have never felt a juvenile as in that moment. And would always be conscious of my actions from then on lest I come across as one again.

You Do Not Mess Around in School Colours
August 8, 1984

Br Pinto was furious. Three boys from class eleven had created a ruckus at Chanakya cinema, getting into fistfights with students of the notorious Khalsa College. The police had to intervene reportedly.

What boys did outside school was their business. Not that the management condoned any unruly behaviour, no matter the provocations. Their crime was being in school uniform when the incident happened. That is what really got the principal riled up. 'Do what you want to, but we will not tolerate anyone bringing dishonour to the school colours,' he told all of us during the morning assembly. 'Take off your belt and tie outside the school gates if you want to be part of any trouble. Whatever justification you give will be unacceptable.'

The three boys got away with a rap on their knuckles, but none of us could expect any leniency in the future. Another lesson learned for life.

Gawking at Women Bathing Out in the Open
September 3, 1984

Why were Joel and Mahijit so animated early morning in the chemistry lab? They had their eyes on women bathing!

There was a construction site adjoining our school and the labour lived in hutments temporarily built there itself. The bath was a makeshift enclosure made of tin sheets. Its top was open to the sky, providing a clear line of sight from our lab. The labourers did not expect their privacy to be violated from above.

The sight of the female skin sent the two boys in a tizzy; we were still curious adolescents not having been intimate with a woman yet. How were the others behaving? A few gawked unabashedly, even as the hypocrites tried to look down furtively. Some were indifferent to it, while those perched on moral high ground scoffed at the desperate behaviour.

Sadly, not much has changed at such construction sites in the country even now. While we uphold the modesty and dignity of the upper classes, those at the bottom of the social rung are treated with scant respect.

Everyone Seeks Mrs Kak's Attention
September 5, 1984

'Mrs Manju Kak will be teaching you history, you're a lucky class.'

If there was someone who could make a subject interesting, it was Mrs Kak. We wanted to be taught by one of the best teachers out there. And perhaps the most beautiful too. The boys were generally infatuated by her.

I would not deny being taken by her but my attraction went deeper than skin. It was the way she illustrated the dynamics of modern world history which drew me in. I was fascinated with the geo-political events of the western world from the late eighteenth century to the mid-nineteenth century. I wanted to be in politics later in life, modelling myself around German leader Otto von Bismarck.

I applied myself to excel in the subject for the love of it and also to impress Mrs Kak. I was not drawn much to ancient Indian history but the syllabus included that too. When covering the Dilwara Temples, the famous Jain temples in Mount Abu in Rajasthan, I considered bringing photos my father had clicked on a visit there when I was in class six. They showed the carvings and architecture in much greater detail than those in the textbooks. By the time I decided to, we had already covered the chapter in our class; I still shared them with Mrs Kak. 'Oh, you should have brought these sooner na,' she said making me feel worse for a chance to look good amongst my classmates. She took them to show to other sections though. I never got the photos back and the gaps in the family albums are still there.

Come Teacher's Day, and one of us had to deliver an address appreciating Mrs Kak's contribution to our education. To my delight, I was selected for the job; I must have manifested it. The headmaster helped me write the speech, but I would stutter at the word 'idiosyncrasies'—I was hearing it for the first time and was unable to pronounce it correctly no matter how many times I rehearsed. I was nervous when I took the stage. Just when the word was about to come up in the speech, there was an interruption; it gave me a few moments to gather my wits and speak the word out correctly. Phew!

Mrs Kak left school after teaching our batch; her husband was in the Indian Foreign Service, and they relocated to Hong Kong. But we would reconnect years later and stay in touch.

Charlie Has a Go at the Whole Class
September 18, 1984

I am still wondering what our collective crime was.

As usual, after the break, all Middle school students assembled in the playgrounds—each class in its own single file—before entering the building one behind the other. As we approached our class, located right opposite the headmaster's office, we were asked to queue up along the wall outside the room. Wonder why? Then Br Fernandes emerged from his office, a scowl on his face, Charlie swinging in his right hand. Not a good sign.

'Go in,' he indicated. But slowly. One at time. Pause at the door. Bend over. Whack, whack. Two blows of the cane on our bums. For each of us. No exceptions. No matter how many times we have been hit, the immunity to pain never sets in. Whacks follow intense rubbing of sore bottoms, some doing it with quiet dignity, others making a show and dance of it hopping like hares with tails on fire.

I made a mistake when it was my turn. For some stupid reason, I allowed my right arm to come in the way of the swinging cane. It was a reflex action, as if I could stop or grab the cane. Result? Not only was I sore behind, but the edge of the cane caught my arm too. Causing a piercing pain and leaving a blue spot on my forearm. That hurt more actually and would take a days to heal. Only I could have managed to self-inflict this wound.

I am still wondering what our collective crime was.

A Missed Opportunity to Foster Citizen Journalism
October 4, 1984

Every democracy needs a free press. As does an 'autocratic' school. A bunch of class eight hacks published a magazine called *EUREKA* and then some from C section in our batch produced *PAGES*. They printed 500 copies each, going classroom to classroom selling them. The editorial direction was provided by Siddhartha Mukherjee and Ashok Rai respectively, who would go on to win the Sword of Honour in their respective batches in class twelve.

It was an exercise in journalism, in business management and in publishing. Curiosity ensured all copies of one edition sold out. They should have persisted with the publications, institutionalizing the process so subsequent batches could have taken over where the previous ones had left off. Just like the school pioneered computer education, it could have been at the forefront of fostering citizen journalism. Br Bennet was all praise for the publishers, calling the experience education in itself.

I was not given the opportunity to participate in these and the school magazine even though I was considering a career in journalism. I did take the initiative and revive the dormant college magazine while studying engineering. I had to follow the conventional path for a while, but I broke free to go back to school for a Masters in Journalism when I was thirty-one and make it a lifelong career, writing for different platforms and media.

Joel Walked Out of Class Because He Was Given the Option To

October 12, 1984

Mrs Kak was at her patience's end; the class would not shut up. 'Whoever does not want to study can leave the class,' she finally said, sternly.

Joel Fernandes decided to be an obedient student for once. He picked up his bag and walked out because, as Mrs Kak had instructed, those who did not want to study could leave the class. That's it.

He was lucky Br Fernandes did not spot him loitering in the corridors. He had no plausible explanation for it; saying Mrs Kak gave him the option to be out would not cut it. Caning was guaranteed in such a scenario.

Indira Gandhi Assassinated
October 31, 1984

It was one of those days when no one forgets where they were and what they were doing when the news came in.

Even before anything was said and done, an unusual silence enveloped the school. Teachers were called out for an unscheduled meeting. Some of us were sent to mind junior classes. I remember standing in class 5-C; I had been told to engage them in some academic exercises but gave up when I realized I was not getting through to anyone. There should have been pandemonium in the absence of any adults, but no one messed around; it's as if there was a collective premonition about a tragedy.

Then the teachers returned and monitors were sent back to their respective classrooms. Mr Pacheco walked in, not his usual self. He tried to write something on the blackboard, then chucked the chalk out of the window. And started muttering, in a style you identified uniquely with him: 'Chey, chey ... they killed her man, they killed her. Those fuckers, they killed her. She's no more. She's gone.'

We were like, what what? Who? 'Prime Minister Indira Gandhi. She's gone. They killed her.' That's how the news was broken to us, much to our shock. Assassinated by two of her guards, both Sikhs, to avenge what they perceived a sacrilege against the Golden Temple during Operation Bluestar. Uncertainty hung in a room of 14-year-olds, figuring what to make of it.

Teaching was suspended for the day. Within an hour, we were told to pack our bags and leave. The school buses had been called in early to take us home. Rahul and Priyanka Gandhi had been whisked within minutes of the shooting; that's how VVIP security drills worked. It was difficult to distinguish rumours from truth. Our only source of information were eighty boys in the bus with no means to communicate with anyone beyond.

Looking out of the windows of the bus, everything seemed normal. But the city would come to a standstill very quickly, as schools and offices shut. My father also came back early. Intuitively, we knew it would be best to lock ourselves indoors.

The state run news broadcasts—the only source of news till newspapers arrived the following morning—would not officially confirm the death until later in the evening, even though there was no denying it. Neighbours gathered, wondering what awaited, everyone an expert on the why of what happened, with opinions of the futures awaiting us.

And then the riots broke.

Locked Up During the Riots
November 1984

For seventy-two hours from the night of the assassination, significant pockets of the country and all of Delhi in particular were hostage to rioters, looters and murderers. Uttering a cry for revenge, they went after the Sikh population. Nothing was spared—places of worship, homes, shops, offices, cars and other property. Around 2,700 were recorded to have been killed, the number much higher if you asked the affected communities. Many more were injured, displaced, their savings and livelihoods lost.

School stayed shut for many days. We were confined indoors, looking out of our windows as fires raged in our immediate neighbourhood too. A new grocery shop, run by an aged Sikh man and his daughter, was reduced to ashes; I used to pick daily supplies from them. Night vigils were set up, but I was not sure how they would have helped. None of us were capable of holding a mob back. Not that our locality was under threat given the demographic of its residents. But we lived in dread anyway; my father's brother was married to a Sikh. My aunt's parents and two young sisters had to be whisked away under cover to a safe house. But there was no sense of security till things had not settled.

Rahul and Priyanka never returned to school. Rajiv Gandhi was sworn in as the prime minister, his youth bringing hope of changes in the country. But he too would be assassinated on May 21, 1991. Investigations into the riots were initiated as expected, cases dragging on for decades. Even though a few were convicted, courts were not presented evidence to proclaim any big guns guilty. It was generally believed the police looked the other way for at least forty-eight hours before calm and order was gradually restored. The Sikhs neither saw any justification in what happened, nor have they felt any subsequent justice was done to console their grieving hearts.

The Prime Minister's Cheese Sandwiches

We shared our tiffins freely, even with grandsons of the prime minister. Rahul Gandhi usually carried cheese sandwiches and we could claim to have had lunch from the kitchen of the first political family of India.

Whether it was his disposition or an expectation of the high and mighty, he was quite reticent in his interactions. Not so on the football field though—his skills were noticed by all, perhaps to do with his half Italian lineage. He was certain to have been a frontline player for the school had his stay not been cut short.

How did he study when confined to home after Indira Gandhi's assassination? Some of his classmates were assigned to share class notes with him. They would be picked and dropped in official cars, seeing him through to his class nine exams before he reportedly moved to Doon School.

Sanjay Sharma Makes History: First Ever to Be Slapped by Mrs Kak
November 22, 1984

'This is the first time I have slapped a student and you should be ashamed of yourself for making me do this,' said Mrs Kak.

Mrs Kak had never been so furious; she was this time, and that too, over a comic act. The class was echoing with yapping boys, testing her patience. Mukul Dev Kaushal egged Sanjay Sharma to mimic Keshto Mukherjee, the Bollywood actor famous for his comic acts in a perpetually intoxicated state. His signature sound in all movies went something like 'eeeeehhh hey,' no words suitable to describe it but try saying it stammering like a sheep. Sanjay did a good imitation of it. Expecting it to be drowned in the din, he let the sound out—at precisely the moment when there was a lull in the room. Everyone heard it loud and funny, bursting into laughter. Except Mrs Kak.

She called him forward and asked what the sound was. Sanjay pleaded it was a hiccup, but Mukul kept heckling to repeat the Keshto Mukherjee act. Finally, he did, for the teacher to slap him in a reflex reaction. It upset her further because she had never slapped a student earlier.

Sanjay Sharma would go down in history to be the first to be slapped by the history teacher.

Jumped in Lake to Save His Life
December 7, 1984

Pavan Uttam got thrashed by Br D'Souza. For 'swimming' in the Badhkal Lake during the annual picnic.

No one felt safe with the section B boys. Their class teacher, Mr Rosemayer, refused to accompany them for the annual class picnic. He was scared of the likes of Akash Dhawan in the class.

No problem. Jitender Mahajan's father owned a transport company and a bus was arranged. Without authorisation and without supervision, the class went off on a picnic to Badhkal Lake. To have the best time of the fourteen years of their lives on the planet.

All was fine till it was time to leave. They needed to be back in school on time to catch their respective school buses home—parents were not aware of the 'unofficial' picnic. Pavan Uttam was still out in a paddle boat with Akash Dhawan; others were making a ruckus from the shore, threatening to leave him behind if he did not make it back quickly. He insisted of returning immediately but Akash urged him to calm down. The latter had come on his Royal Enfield bike separately and offered to drop Pavan back. 'No way, I will get into trouble. Either with the cops for underage riding or with my folks or both,' Pavan said, on the verge of losing his temper.

With Akash not cooperating, Pavan had no choice but to jump into the cold water to wade back. By then, the management and staff of the lake had gathered too, and caught hold of Pavan for dangerous swimming. Despite all pleas and requests—and tears—by the boys, the authorities would not give in. They finally called the school to report on the boys before letting them leave.

Br D'Souza was waiting at the school gate when they returned but no action was taken immediately. Pavan Uttam was called out in the assembly the following morning and caned for the Middle School to see. Not just for going on a picnic without permission and for risking his life, but also for tarnishing the reputation of St. Columba's School.

Cracked Code to Win Unlimited Televisions. Only to Throw It.

December 13, 1984

Talk about a wasting the 'genius' in me to procrastination.

Ms Khosla won a television set through a monthly competition in a magazine. The competition organizers gave a long word and you had to make as many words as you could using the letters in the word. The one who submitted the maximum number of valid words would be declared winner.

I made a computer program that gave me all combinations possible. All I had to do after that was scratch ineligible words and double check the rest in the dictionary. I could win a television every month. But no. After all the smart work, I played dumb and did not enter the competition. I could have opened a shop selling television sets with my winnings.

The program was a gift to myself on my birthday, but I literally threw it away. It seems to be a trait in me. I come close to achieving or completing something only for inertia to set in, wasting all the effort put in. If you are reading this, then you know I have finally broken free of such patterns.

1984: Not a Year to be Forgotten

This was the year when Indians shone amongst the stars yet also plummeted to the depths of collective shame.

Squadron Leader Rakesh Sharma became the first Indian to be launched into space aboard the Soyuz T-11. The nation tuned in when his call with Indira Gandhi was telecast. When the prime minister asked how India looked from space, all hearts swelled with patriotic pride when he promptly replied, '*saare jahan se achchaa* (better than the rest of the world).'

The same hearts broke when P.T. Usha missed the bronze medal by one-hundredth of a second in the 400 metres hurdle competition in the Olympic Games, Los Angeles. If her nose had been just a bit longer, she would have been ahead in the photo finish according to some commentators. She was expected to go one better than Milkha Singh's famous fourth place finish in the 400 metres final in the 1960 Olympics in Rome.

In between the two events, Bachendri Pal stood at the top of the world: the first Indian woman to scale the Mount Everest.

What seemed a political footnote at the time but would define caste-based politics in years to follow, Kanshi Ram founded the Bahujan Samaj Party to represent the rights of historically supressed castes in the country. However, a more significant event would change the political landscape permanently: Indira Gandhi gave the go-ahead to Operation Blue Star, permitting Indian troops to storm the Golden Temple in Amritsar to flush out terrorists reportedly holed inside. The intent was to bring an end to the separatist movement for Punjab to be an independent country, but many did not take kindly to an attack on their holiest shrine. No one could claim to distinguish between right and wrong in the proverbial fog of war and Indira Gandhi was assassinated a few months after by her Sikh guards.

The year ended in further tragedy with the infamous Bhopal gas tragedy. Methyl isocyanate leaked out from the Union Carbide pesticide plant, exposing a dense population of over half a million to it. While over 2,000 people died instantly, estimates of deaths in the coming weeks and years go up to as high as 20,000. Tens of thousands suffered injuries and illnesses, none of the records claiming authority in accuracy. The expatriate management literally got away with murder by being allowed to leave the country without trial, never to be extradited back.

Our Generation at the Forefront of the Great Transition
January 1, 1985

The year gone by was one the most tragic in India's history. But the new year was one of hope, one of anticipation. There was optimism in the air. The country had a new prime minister, the youngest ever, Rajiv Gandhi—an alumnus of St. Columba's. The nation was counting on him to leverage his unprecedented three quarters majority in the Lok Sabha to bring in much needed reforms—social and economic.

Winds of change had been blowing across the world and it was a matter of time before India too would be swept up in a gale. Rajiv Gandhi was in the right place at the right time and could have been the catalysing force, if only he would have done the right things. Irrespective of who led the change, they would have to rely on our generation to power it.

Because we would take the baton from a generation of an old India and pass it onto the generation of the twenty first century. We would thus be the only ones who would have lived in the past, built a new present and provided a foundation for the future.

We knew scarcity. We knew what it was to be a society of the middle class and the poor, the wealthy being an exception. Unless you came with the advantage of a certain background, it was extremely difficult to break into the upper ranks, so protected the privileged kept their domain.

We have known simpler times. With not much to aspire for, bonds with friends and family were our assets. Joy lay in reading, sharing stories, home-cooked meals, playing in the park. We grew vegetables in the kitchen garden, climbed trees to stay cool in the summers, connected our tape recorders to make endless copies of music and slept under the starry skies. We were at ease with what we had. We did not fret if opportunities in the country offered only more of the same.

And then things started changing. At a good speed in the 1980s when we were in school, and at supersonic speed in the 1990s when we were entering the workforce. We could handle it, adjust to it. We did not suffer from vertigo because we were grounded in our outlook and we had supreme faith in our abilities because of the education we had received.

Rajiv Gandhi brought in controlled liberalisation, technology being the priority sector. India's famed software industry took its baby steps, not taking too long to grow up. The outsourcing and offshoring industries followed. Millions felt they could sleep sound when peace accords in Assam, Sri Lanka and Punjab were signed. The seeds of friendship between India and Pakistan were sowed with young prime ministers—Rajiv Gandhi and Benazir Bhutto—on either side of the border ; it is a pity we are yet to see the blossoms.

Political headwinds blurred Rajiv Gandhi's vision of building a modern economy, the task to be taken on by Prime Minister P.V. Narasimha Rao and his brilliant finance minister, Manmohan Singh, after his assassination. They brought in the guillotine as the only way to usher in a revolution. They liberalised the rules of the game to truly democratise the economy, releasing the stranglehold a few had over production through the notorious 'licence raj.'

The change was almost dramatic overnight. Demand for talent zoomed. Many of us earned more in the first months of our jobs than what our fathers were earning annually after putting in three decades of work. There was an exponential rise in wealth, jobs, investments, infrastructure and even the population. Our generation would be the one driving it with our education, youth, energy and ideas.

Unfortunately, there was a recklessness to the growth story. Even as glitzy offices and opulent homes came up, the natural world suffered. Ancient forests were cut down, the disruption of biodiversity endangering the health of the planet and humans. Species went extinct. The air became polluted, water toxic, food infested with pesticides. Rivers dried, landfills became unmanageable mountains. No one cared. No one cares. We turned deaf to cries of environmentalists, our eyes too blinded by glitz to see the state of the world around us.

We would be the first generation in India to bring in unimaginable prosperity and also to wreak immeasurable havoc.

Our formative years were of material deficits, yet our heads always felt light and free. Our children have only known surfeit and yet suffer from a mental health epidemic.

Why would they not? We lived in slow times, sauntering and loitering our way to pick up a Colgate from the market. Now we hyperventilate if it takes longer than ten minutes to deliver. Our phones would go unanswered (if they connected at all) and we would not know who had called; we become impatient if our text is not replied to within minutes, if not seconds. We travel, not to treat our five senses, but to get likes on social media. We seek the world's approval and validation, deliberately making them a part of our private lives. Then get distressed when ours pale in comparison to theirs.

We initially sought money to provide comfort and security, now we make money to feed our egos, refusing to get off the treadmill and step out to feel the grass under our feet, to chase butterflies, to read a book under a tree and to lie on our back counting the stars in the sky.

Our generation was at the forefront of the great transition. Where we took ourselves? That is for future historians to analyse and judge.

Collateral Damage: When Charlie Struck the Wrong Ones

February 15, 1985

Br Fernandes was furious. He could hear a loud ululating sound emanate from one of the basement classrooms, the pattern repeating every few minutes. Unable to concentrate, he felt it was time for action. He found confusion reigning in the craft class, with the hapless teacher making vain attempts to gain control. Without further ado, the entire class was punished.

Having returned to the office, he heard the same wailing sound from the basement. On investigation, the craft class was silent and busy. However, in the next classroom, the elocution teacher Mrs Haider was putting the boys through the paces of a piece called, *'The Wind in the Woods!'*

Oops! Br Fernandes was embarrassed for acting in haste. But at least order was restored in the crafts class, even if due to collateral damage.

How Do You Remove Chewed Gum from Your Hair?

February 4, 1985

Someone stuck chewing gum is Mrs Mathias' hair. She was upset. Br Pinto was livid.

'If the culprits did not confess, or if their friends did not squeal on them, all of 9-D would be caned.' A coward snitched three names. When interrogated, they admitted to what they called a harmless 'prank.'

They were first slapped on their faces. Then caned on their hands. Followed by whacks on the backside. It was Charlie's lucky day. Could not be said for some of my classmates.

I doubt if the three ever chewed gum again.

How the 'Grinch' Stole the Chemistry Lab
February 15, 1985

Final exams were just days away, stressing our nervous system as usual. All things science only made it worse for me, so I decided to visit Vineet Kohli at home. To confirm certain rumours doing the rounds.

And they were true. He had set up a chemistry lab in his study. Built from stuff stolen from school. He had everything except the gas supply. Even big beakers and the Bunsen burner; how did he walk out with them?

Since he had set up a lab, I could practice for my exam here. But it came with was a risk. There was no supervision of anyone knowledgeable. If any formula went awry, we could set the house on fire or choke on toxic fumes. I fiddled with some chemicals, realized it was not really helping my preparations, and left Vineet to experiment till he found his Eureka! moment.

Vineet managed to survive the lab at home and went on to make himself fabulously rich in the world of finance. Three decades on, we urged him to donate a modern lab to the school and thus pay back for the stolen goods with interest and penalty. It would cost him the equivalent of loose change. When last checked, he was non-committal to the cause.

Shahrukh Khan Wins the Sword of Honour. And Then Stands Up for Its Honour.

February 22, 1985

It's official. Shah Rukh Khan will be awarded the Sword of Honour. No surprises there. He was probably in line for it since junior school. I don't think any of his batchmates had any delusions they could pip him to it. He was on top of theatre, cricket, football, hockey and other extra-curriculars. He scored 80 per cent in the boards, topping in electronics in his class.

When making a case for admission to the prestigious St. Stephen's College, he underscored his credentials by mentioning the Sword of Honour. The board said it does not count when considering his candidature. He got miffed at the disrespect for his school and walked out to enrol in Hansraj College. Is this a true story? Likely. Because it was quite talked about at the time.

Computer Studies to Feature in the Boards for the First Time

March 18, 1985

For the first time ever, students in India would be appearing for a board exam in Computer Studies. The only institution to feature in this historical footnote would be St. Columba's School. Those senior to us would be taking the exam, while we would the following year.

A report in *The Times of India* said, 'The only school that seems to know what it is doing is St. Columba's where computers were introduced four years ago. This year, fifty children have taken computers as a subject in their Indian School Certificate Examination.'

Other schools tried to emulate our achievement. We paid no additional fee but some of my cousins had to for this elective subject. Yet, their program had syntax errors and it would be a while before they managed to debug it and deliver students their due.

Someone Will Drink the Yuckiest Mocktail if the Money is Good
March 28, 1985

Take a glass three quarters full of water. Add substantial doses of tomato ketchup, mustard, chili flakes, oregano, salt, pepper and lemon. Stir well. Announce a bounty of Rs 10 to anyone who drinks it. It was a safe bet. Who would down such a concoction, obnoxious in appearance and in taste?

Manav Abrol would. He emptied the contents in one swig. I supposed he had to do it this way; had he taken a break, he might not have been able to get himself to drink the rest. I felt like throwing up just looking at him. We pooled in to pony up the reward; he deserved a tip for actually doing it.

This was a game groups of students occasionally played at Nirula's, the only of its kind fast food chain in town. Invariably, we would go there to celebrate the end of exams and watch a movie at Chanakya cinema located in the same building. It was a treat we received additional pocket money for twice a year.

Still wondering: Did Manav do it for the money or for the thrill of it?

Sanjay Sharma is a 'Goonda'
March 30, 1985

Sanjay Shama's father had never attended a Parent Teacher Meeting, it was his mother who had to bear the indignity of being told of her son's exploits for ten years. But this time Mrs Thomas insisted on the father making an appearance.

Father and son came in on the appointed day, two big men walking to the inquest on either side of the corridor, like two tigers staying clear of each other's territories. No sooner did they enter the classroom when Mrs Thomas closed her eyes, covering them with her fists, letting out a dramatic cry, 'Your son is a *goonda* Mr Sharma.' Regaining her composure after a few seconds, she gave the complete low-down on the younger Sharma's exploits, describing him no less than a goon. The men stayed stoic as she ranted. The elder assured her an iron fist would henceforth be used, the 'child' promising to behave himself. Both lied.

They went back the way they had come, at safe distance, before junior got the worst blasting of his life at home. But it was not enough to get through his thick skin. Sanjay Sharma would be responsible for more nervous breakdowns amongst staff before he was done with school.

I Finish First in Class. A First.
March 30, 1985

I did it. I topped my class for the first time ever. In class nine.

Venkataram Krishnaswamy, who had won the equivalent of the academic gold medal more than anyone else over the years, was second. But he was muttering: he lost out because I had an advantage in Hindi being from north India; he did not being from down south.

'Hello?' I wanted to argue back. 'This never came up earlier. Anyway, if my strong suit was Hindi, weren't those from his region naturally gifted in mathematics and science? And his family conversed and read more in English than mine did. Don't be a bad sport,' I wanted to say but I let it pass. I was soaking in the moment!

I was on top of the world. For once. And not for the last time.

Entered Class Ten: The Big Boys of Middle School
April 2, 1985

A new academic year and we were the seniormost class in Middle School. It will also be our last year in this building before we move to Senior School and under the direct supervision of the principal himself.

This will be a year we appear for the boards and choose what we want to study in the final two years of school. While everyone else moves rooms, we stayed in the same. The sign on the door was changed from 9-D to 10-D because Br Fernandes, the headmaster, was to remain our class teacher and we needed to be close to his office so he could discharge his other responsibilities efficiently.

We were the big boys of Middle School!

End of the Team of Shahrukh Khan, Vivek Razdan and Rahul Dev Kaushal
April 8, 1985

There was a time when three superstars of the future took to the field together, representing St. Columba's School in cricket.

Shahrukh Khan would go on to become the king of Bollywood. Rahul Dev would be a household name as a model and an actor in both Hindi and south Indian language films. Vivek Razdan would go on to play for India and also become a face everyone would recognize as a commentator on television. We would be looking at all three on a screen.

Shahrukh graduated this year. Vivek moved to Sardar Patel School to improve his prospects as a professional cricketer; the school was a nursery for many a talented sportsman. Rahul would stay on, in his final year in school.

Br Pinto was quite disappointed, even miffed, when Vivek decided to migrate. Despite his low grades, the principal had made an exception and offered him subjects of his choice in the eleventh. Vivek had made it a condition to stay on in Columba's but changed his mind later.

He may have made the right choice. For us, he will always be a Columban!

Commodore 64: A Computer of My Own

April 17, 1985

I got my reward for finishing first in class—a Commodore 64 computer of my own. Possible because my father's job required him to travel overseas regularly.

The keyboard and the processor were within the same casing, with the option of using the television as the screen instead of a dedicated monitor. Over time I got an external floppy drive and a dot matrix printer too. Let's not forget they were pricey acquisitions at the time for someone on a government salary. My father could afford it only because he was paid an additional dollar allowance while travelling.

My programming went into an overdrive thereon. I did not have to rely on limited time available on the school's computers. I was literally in my private lab, experimenting with different programs, loving it like no other subject. For the boards, we had to sit on computers to be tested; I was allowed to take my Commodore 64 and the unwieldy television to school—much to the puzzlement of students and staff alike.

The computer came with a game, Football, in a cartridge you plugged in. With a joystick to move players. Before long, I was making fantasy leagues and pitting teams against one another. The Football World Cup 1986 was being played in Mexico during the summer break following the class ten boards; I went into an overdrive then. I would watch matches live all night and mimic the World Cup on my computer by playing the same teams against each other. You could not call me a soothsayer because my scores did not necessarily predict those of the real matches.

I realized my brain is wired to be a good coder yet I did not make a career in information technology. I would have entered just when the industry was taking off globally, surfing to the top like my peers did. Wonder what could have been had I made different choices?

But then again, my psyche is wired to explore ideas; I would not have stayed long enough in the software industry.

A Columban Loses His Parents in Air India Bombing
June 24, 1985

The front pages of every newspaper screamed the same headline: 329 Killed as Air India Plane Plunges Into the Atlantic Ocean.

Air India Flight 182, a Boeing 747 named Kanishka, en-route Montreal to London, exploded mid-air and crashed into the waters off the coast of Ireland the previous day. Sikh separatists were suspected to have planted a bomb on the plane going by the circumstantial evidence available immediately. The conspiracy would never be unravelled fully.

Tragically, one of our own lost his parents who were on the way back home from Canada. The school respected his privacy and fragile emotional state by saying little publicly.

Mr Sood's Slaps Feared by the Bravest

No one slapped like Mr Sood. It could bring even those with the thickest skin to their knees. He had a patented technique for maximum destruction.

First, he brought his palm within inches of your cheek, perfectly parallel. It would then be spiked with a dose of kinetic energy. A sudden movement and the sound of a slap would follow. It was a blur to even the keenest eye, leaving a burning cheek in its wake. Being a teacher in the physics laboratory, he was applying principles of mass, energy and velocity to desired effect.

The slaps were painful no doubt but also disgusting considering where his hands tended to wander. When he was not using them for experiments, writing on the blackboard or for slapping, they would be employed for scratching his balls (Calling them testicles may be politically decent but it changes their character!). Strangely, whenever he did, his trousers slid down a bit; we wanted to pool in to buy him suspenders lest he ends up exposing any ugliness below the waist.

Br Fernandes Gets Nostalgic
July 12,1985

We were sitting in Br Fernandes' office after school, eight boys and a headmaster conversing about everything under the sun like one would as a family at home. It was much cooler in here than even back home. Not sure what the trigger was but the headmaster got nostalgic, going back to the time when he himself was a little boy. In his words:

'My two elder brothers and I joined St. Columba's in 1951, just ten years after it had been built. The admission process was a far cry from what it is today. The Principal, Br J.J. Crease, an Englishman, warmly welcomed our family to his office. This was a small room adjoining the foyer accommodating the principal's desk, a clerk, a few chairs and almirahs.

A happy, gentle soul, Br Crease was new to Delhi, having spent his early years as a Brother in St. Aloysius' School in Quilon in Kerala. He graciously offered us seats and after a few preliminary questions, jotted down our names on the back of an old envelope. He then mentioned the classes to which we were to be admitted and the date of the opening of school. That was it! This 'system' no doubt, would lead to chaos and confusion.

At the time, St. Columba's comprised a single red-brick building which is as impressive today as it was then. This housed most of the classrooms, laboratories and Brothers' residential quarters; it would eventually become the Senior School. A garage at the back sheltered a large Chevrolet van with a wood-panelled body.

A few days before classes began, the clerks realised that there were far more pupils than the structure could accommodate. As a pro tem measure, my classroom in class one was the garage, the entrance foyer was given to class two and sturdy tents erected around the field for those in third.

While the garage and the foyer offered a modicum of scholastic environment, the tents did not. The desks and an old blackboard resting on an easel were the only features which indicated some sort of learning space. Yet, the teachers and the boys somehow enjoyed studying in an environment quite exposed to the elements. Though the roof of the tent was doubled-layered, the sides were protected by canvas sheets which flapped away in the wind and afforded little protection during the monsoons. Three stocky boys were commissioned to retrieve the blackboard each time it was blown to the ground. Amazingly, none of the boys and their parents ever raised any objections. A similar situation today would probably warrant at least a governmental enquiry!

All this while, a fine three-storied Junior School building was being constructed on the far side of the field; two floors of classrooms with an auditorium at the top. In a year or so, Junior classes moved into bright, new classrooms.

I left St. Columba's in 1961 to finish my schooling in Goethals Memorial School, Kurseong, near Darjeeling. It was also the beginning of my training as a Christian Brother. I taught in different schools across the country before being appointed your headmaster.'

Random Act: Slapped by a 'Sardar' on the Road
July 27, 1985

We were walking back from Chanakya cinema to catch a bus home when we spotted a group of boys coming from the opposite side. This isn't a problem, until one makes it. The heftiest of them, a sardar (Sikh) in a bright red turban, suddenly stopped, gave me a tight slap, and resumed walking. No provocation, no interaction—just like that.

I almost fell to the ground and I still recall Anish's words muttered while my head was trying to restore equilibrium: 'The look on your face invites such behaviour.' He made as little sense as the idiot who struck me.

It was a bitter end to a birthday ritual we followed for years. Manav and Jayant had their birthdays two days apart in July, while Anish and I in January and December respectively. We would go out for birthday celebrations twice—where two pooled in to treat the others. We were returning from a meal at Nirula's and movie at Chanakya, paid for by the July birthday boys, when this incident happened.

None of us had it in us to fight back and let the matter be. I would see the same Sikh a few days later at Celesta, the inter-school music competition hosted by our school. He was trying to impress girls from Carmel Convent; I wanted to warn the girls but chose personal safety over any nobility. I darted away before he could spot me. I doubt if he would have recognized me even if our eyes had met. But he might have slapped me again because, as Anish said, the look on my face provokes such behaviour.

Bird Watching

Columbans would do anything to catch a sight of girls from other schools. The 'bird watching', as we called it, would not lead to any close encounters but the sport still tickled us in some parts. How did we pursue this activity?

From the Bus on the Way to School in the Morning

Our school had done one good thing: we started about fifteen minutes before others. All the girls would be waiting at their bus stops as we whizzed by. Looking at us making the usual monkey of ourselves by waving—and sometimes calling out—at them.

A good look would require a risk to life and limb: there would be a jostle to 'hang out' from the footboard of the doorless bus, with seniority assigning rights. Sticking heads out of windows was for lower classes. It is fortunate no accident has ever been reported.

Freezing winters, stifling summers or wet monsoons—no matter the weather, there was always a set of boys who would brave it to gawk at girls from Mater Dei, CJM, Loreto and Carmel.

Peeping Into the Headmaster's Offices

Girls from other schools would sometimes visit for official purposes, like inviting us for school events. It never took long for news to spread and we would pop by the headmaster's office for reasons invented on the spot. Including to check if the headmaster was in. What we were really doing was checking girls out with slanted eyes; we were required to report back on the quality of our sightings to those waiting back in the classroom.

Being Sent to Schools with Girls

There were times when we were sent to other schools. The lucky 'bastards' chosen had a whale of a time—they had the full school to feast their eyes on. Interestingly, students from all-girls schools would develop a need to check if the principal was in when any of us were seated in the waiting area.

Events Hosted by School

This was fertile ground—the auditorium or field would be packed with girls from other schools. Of particular interest were those from St. Thomas School; they were infamous for occupying front row seats, in skirts shorter than of those from any other schools, legs as suggestively apart as possible. They were not required to wear divided skirts like in CJM. Maybe it was a strategy to distract competition so their own schoolmates could win.

If It's Celesta, It Has to Rain
August 10, 1985

If anyone wanted the heavens to open up, they could either perform a rain dance or organize Celesta.

Columba's hosted an inter-school western school competition annually in the Middle School grounds for a few years—and it rained each time. Only for the skies to clear in time so the music could play, and kids could rock.

That's what happened in the first edition too. Rains delayed the proceedings, leaving band members and attendees drenched. We waited hours for the sun to break up the clouds, and it eventually did—for one of the most memorable evenings we would ever witness in school.

All the boys had a good time for another reason though. Girls from Mater Dei, St. Thomas, Loreto and CJM were in their school uniforms. Their white shirts had become translucent when wet and we could not keep ourselves from ogling at them, curiosity intensifying in our hormone-addled brain. We were a school of 3,000 boys, mostly kept away from interactions with the opposite sex. Looking back, I cringe at our perverse behaviour even though we found no fault in it back then.

Vincent Hughes, the strongest and scariest amongst us, boasting unusually high testosterone levels, was forced to play good cop on the day. Susanne, a visiting student, was wearing a white shirt with no layers underneath. Drenched, her skin was showing through, every eye following her. Of all the people, she went up to Vincent requesting that he guide her to a room where she could change. He took her to class 5-A on the ground floor, stood guard till she came out, escorted her back, and that was it.

The intimacy of the situation gave Vincent palpitations, changing the colour of his face as evidence of what he was going through. However, he swore on his mother he did not even peek into the room nor allow anyone else to. The occasion demanded him to be a gentleman, and that's what he demonstrated.

The field was transformed overnight. Not a blade of grass survived with thousands skidding and dancing on the wet ground. It would take weeks (and lots of money!) to restore the grass. The school discontinued the event after three editions.

I set up a gig organizing events while in college to make additional pocket money. I took permission to organize Celesta and share any profits I made with the school. I did so very successfully, once at the school itself and twice at the Ambedkar Stadium where professional football matches are played. And it rained each time!

Broken Bones Killed a Fledgling Sport
August 20, 1985

There's a new game in town: Rugby Unplugged. Incubated in the Middle School grounds, it was apt to develop into a national sport in our society like ours. Only if Sameer Sharma had not broken his arm.

The sport had no rules governing it. During the break, sections B and E would face off in the field. Any number could join in; more than thirty would for each team daily. They looked more like mobs warming up for a riot than for a game. The equipment was just one tennis ball, fattened by wrapping as many handkerchiefs and rags available.

There was only one objective: score. Did not matter how you got the ball, how you made your way through, who you struck, who struck you. 'The game must go on even if someone died' was the understanding. It was a wild sight, the two sides lunging at each other. Sense dictated you stay out of their way.

Something had to give and it was Sameer's arm. The heftiest guy on the field, he never ran with the ball. He just strode to the opposition goal once he had possession of the ball, aware only a fool would dare to tackle him. George seemed to have taken the field with a death wish; rather than take Sameer head on, he stretched his foot to trip him. It worked and Sameer broke his arm. Had the tactic not worked, George would have ended up with broken ribs.

Either way, it was a day when some bones had to break. And it was enough for Br Fernandes to ban the sport. For a long time, the field would hear no battle cries, see no blood spilled.

The School Nurturing Decent Human Beings

Double, double toil and trouble;
Fire burn and cauldron bubble.
Fillet of a fenny snake,
In the cauldron boil and bake;
Eye of newt and toe of frog,
Wool of bat and tongue of dog,
Adder's fork and blind-worm's sting,
Lizard's leg and howlet's wing,
For a charm of powerful trouble,
Like a hell-broth boil and bubble.
Double, double toil and trouble;
Fire burn and cauldron bubble.

Cool it with a baboon's blood,
Then the charm is firm and good.

You would expect a place like St. Columba's to be a favourite of the three witches from *The Tragedy of Macbeth,* brewing a potion of toxic masculinity in a school of three thousand boys, their hormones in a churn. Thwarting them were the Brothers and teachers, who were focused on making decent human beings of us, nice guys everyone would want to know.

We were bright, the quality of education was the highest and we were sitting in the centre of the country, exposed to whatever we needed to be prepared to face the world. We could have been taught to kill it, but we were groomed to protect it. Save a value system that is nation agnostic, that is class, race, colour, religion and economic status agnostic. St. Columba's did not need to train us to be capitalists or politicians chasing seats at the apex of the power pyramid. Rather, it took upon itself the responsibility of making tolerant, generous, kind human beings of us.

Yes, the school was strict. Transgressions were not dealt with lightly; we were counselled, we were scolded, we were 'Charlie-d.' But none of us felt bitter about it, none of us felt violated. We knew the place our teachers were coming from—one of making better versions of ourselves. They led by example. And that is why they commanded the respect, the awe that they did. They loved us without bias. They did not care for nor were impressed by power or wealth but with your scores and behaviour.

And it shows. When you meet a Columban, you sense he is one even before introducing himself. Because he is a gentle soul, a humble man, a likeable fellow.

You Don't Lose to Teachers to Show Respect
September 5, 1985

The boys did not get too many opportunities to give it back to their tutors, but an opportunity was upon them. On the hockey field. In a match between staff and prefects to mark Teachers' Day. With many of these prefects also on the school team, it was expected to be a no-contest.

It was. Only someone flipped the narrative. The scoreline read 6-1 in favour of teachers—evidence we still had a lot to learn from them. Spin doctors were called in as a face-saver for prefects. 'We deliberately lost out of respect for our masters,' they said. Not sure if anyone bought into the propaganda.

Those who did, rubbished it when the boys 'thrashed' teachers on the basketball court on the last day of school before the winter break. Of course, it wasn't one-sided all through. Teachers took the early lead, credit going to Br 'T.A.L.L.' Pinto, Br 'F.A.S.T.' Fernandes and Mr 'H.A.R.D.Y.' Rocha as the commentators put it. The boys had also just come out of the last of the mid-term exams and were still seeing the ball as rectangular text books. Once warmed up though, the boys grabbed the ball and did not let it go. To emerge runaway winners. To hell with respect!

Were We an Elite School?

'Our salaries are lower than offered in other private schools in the city.'

Why would Mr Peter Rocha say this if we were considered an elite school? Because we were not elite economically. While we had a few rich kids, most of us came from families living pay cheque to pay cheque. The school had no frills and everyone was treated the same no matter who you were. One of the teachers even rapped Rahul Gandhi on his head for behaving like a dolt, asking if his brain was full of spaghetti!

We were elite in values. In educational standards. To foster decency. So, ours may be a better planet to live in. With empathy towards others. Including living and inanimate creations of nature, because everything is sentient whether we accept it or not. How many schools would have Moral Science as a period? To direct us down the path of honourable conduct. In our personal lives and when dealing with the world at large.

Given its popularity, it would have been very easy for St. Columba's to cater primarily to sons of the rich and the influential. They would have paid any fee demanded, enabling the school to compensate its teachers handsomely. They could thus have attracted anyone to work in the school. Even if humility was a casualty.

Because that's what our teachers were: modest, simple, grounded. Earning enough to take care of their families. Putting in that little extra effort, by way of private tuitions mostly, so they could indulge in a cherry once in a while. It would not have been easy for them, to get by with what they were making when other schools would have compensated them far more handsomely. But they would not be anywhere else but in a school like St. Columba's.

We may have had names for them, we may have addressed them disrespectfully once out of earshot. We may have despised some for being strict, for being demanding academically, for punishing our wanton ways. But they stayed put, committed to what they had set out to do. Despite being fully aware of how students spoke about them, of them. They were not ignorant, they chose to selectively ignore.

The dividends were only ours to reap. Most of us went on to pursue careers where we would be earning many times in a month of what teachers earned in a year. Whenever we visited our school or encountered those teachers elsewhere, they would be where they always were. Still dressed simply, still maintaining modest lifestyles. Focused on imparting 'elite' education. To boys who came from marginalised backgrounds, from families financially challenged. Those who needed schools like St. Columba's to be able to overcome their constraints. Under the care of faculty who knew if they did not do what they do, no one else would.

Financial elitism is ephemeral. Values endure.

When Will We Learn Not to Mess with Mrs Rebello?

September 10, 1985

With less than six months to go for the boards, Mrs Rebello lost it. She walked out of section C to Br Fernandes' office, refusing to teach not just C but the whole batch.

In situations like these, do headmasters wonder why they chose the occupation they did? Their sense of altruism could have found other important causes. But in that moment, there was a responsibility to be discharged, a decision to be taken.

The errant class had to be taught a lesson and thus deterring others from reckless behaviour themselves. For the next two weeks, section C was made to stand in the field during the scheduled biology class. Only when the sun got to them, and they apologised profusely, were they allowed back.

Not that there was any remorse, individually or collectively. The apology was fooling no one. But the situation had to be defused, and teaching resumed. No one wanted to have more of these boys by detaining them.

Of all the teachers, why did we insist on riling Mrs Rebello up? Or did we treat everyone the same, only her fuse was shorter?

No Rum? No Ride for Ms Khosla.

October 7, 1985

There was no English class. Because a bus driver was in an edgy mood. What's the connection?

Ms Khosla had a reputation for being late to the bus stop in the mornings. The driver of Z8, Hukum Singh, would honk patiently till she arrived—even if it meant everyone got late to school, attracting glares from the principal.

But on this day, not only did he arrive two minutes earlier than scheduled, he picked the boys in a hurry and drove off without even looking if anyone was making a dash to catch the bus. What was upsetting him? Everyone knew Ms Khosla supplied him with Old Monk rum—she could access it cheap from the Army canteen—but she had been lax about it lately. He thus had a dry weekend and his grumpy self took it out on her.

Turns out this was not the first time they have had this pow-wow and wouldn't be the last. Suited us—our week got off to a perfect start with a free period.

A Star is Born at Celesta
November 3, 1985

Julius Packiam sent the crowds into a frenzy. His was the most distinctive voice on the school's music circuit. The lead singer of our school band, the star was born on the night of Celesta, the inter-school western music competition. The trophy was his for the taking but as policy, we did not award it to ourselves as hosts.

He became the talk of the town—he had to be. But I discovered a secret—and confronted him. To his credit, he had no hesitation in telling me about it. One of the judges, Loy Mendonsa, invited him to jam with the boys of Mount

St. Mary's, our fiercest 'rival' school. Julius accepted. He would go across to MSM after school, take off his own school tie and belt and practice with them. One of the drummers, Krishnakumar Kunnath, who was also a very good singer, was gracious enough to let Julius be the lead.

Julius did not intentionally keep in clandestine, but it just never came up! He did not go out of the way advertising it but had no qualms in talking about it. He was in it for the camaraderie and the art.

Julius transferred to Columba's in class eleven, having studied in St. Xavier's and Don Bosco prior to this. Admission to a school with a legacy like ours meant to a lot to him. And yet, he never felt intimidated when here, relishing the welcome he received. His initial claim to fame was representing the school in cricket before being discovered as a musician. He followed the MSM band members to Kirorimal College where they continued making music together. Krishnakumar Kunnath would go on to become a famous Bollywood singer, popularly known as KK; he would pass aged fifty-three only. Loy Mendonsa would gain fame—and awards—as a music composer, individually and as a part of the famous Shankar–Ehsaan–Loy trio. Julius would (deservedly) go on to make a career in music, composing scores for Bollywood movies.

My First Shave!
December 13, 1985

Have you ever wondered what a Pomeranian pup would look like if you were to shave his face? You could have seen me on the morning of my sixteenth birthday and visualised. Because that's what I looked like after my first shave.

An uncle who was visiting commented I looked better with the half fertile adolescent moustache I had earlier; he was biased because he always sported a bush on his upper lip. My friends Anish and Manav—who met for the customary birthday lunch—laughed their heads off at my sight. But I could sense they were just forcing themselves to take a dig at my look. They can all go to hell.

When I see my old photographs, I did look like a plucked overgrown baby after the shave. But I looked worse before it. I never sported facial hair. And am glad for it.

Why Would Ashish Gulati Show Off His 'Size'?
January 22, 1986

Breaking news: Ashish Gulati shows off the size of his pecker.

What the hell was that? Ashish unzipped himself in class to show Manav Abrol what a big one he has. 'What the fuck,' Manav said. 'I don't care.'

But word did get around. That Ashish is a dick.

Many boys were obsessed with their size. And would measure themselves with a foot ruler and share the findings even if no one was interested. Was the scale ever washed after use?

How Can We Decide the Course of Our Life at Fifteen?

Most fifty-year-olds cannot provide a convincing answer to why they are doing what they are doing. How can our system expect us to make life defining choices when we are fifteen?

School is a cocoon, a protected environment keeping realities of the world at bay. Yet we are sent down academic paths in high school determining what we study in university, further narrowing our career options. There are barely any reference points for us to make these decisions and before we realize it, we are a part of a herd moving along to conform to a system profiting a select few.

We should have been offered a chance to travel, to work, to pick up vocational courses during and after school. We would have met people from different walks of life, we would have seen how the world operates. We could then have spotted placeholders for different ways to lead this life and identified one where we felt we belonged. By distilling our thoughts, we could align our interests and temperament to doing what we should be doing rather than becoming another sheep in the herd.

But we allow ourselves to be conditioned by those whose world views are limited even if they intend only the best of us. Our parents and peers make us measure success and material gains using their metrics, rather than helping us figure out where contentment lies. Somewhere in this process, we break our linkage with the natural world, we lose our empathy to become agents of a larger good. We cloister ourselves in structures painted gold and silver instead of being out in the open coloured green and blue.

To make things worse, we are sucked into a merit-based class system with its warped logic. The brightest usually study science in school and by extension pick engineering and medicine in university. The next rung, with exceptions, go for economics and commerce. Those who performed poorest are forced to study history and literature! For God's sake, I wanted to study these subjects but those who finish amongst the toppers could not be seen sitting in the class of 'laggards.' Yes, systems are becoming more flexible allowing you to choose your subjects, but you stick to the formula largely. Because you will run into walls where those who experiment may not be favoured for certain courses and jobs.

I wish schools introduced a subject called 'Dreamers.' So, we may imagine possible lives we would rather lead. By being allowed to go into the laboratory called life, mix a few chemicals and analyse the results. So, dreams are not whims but based on substance.

And that would require greater exposure to books, ideas, people and places. You never know what surprises lie in store, what Eureka moments may emerge. Just this journey of discovery may make you do what I chose to: becoming a life scientist, not settled on one set of results, always seeking, always living new lives.

Faith Does Not Allow Dissection in Biology

February 13, 1986

KVK Vikram had been pleading with the principal and the biology teacher: he will not dissect dead cockroaches and frogs!

His family belonged to the Radha Soami sect requiring, amongst other things, a strictly vegetarian life and respect for life. They consume milk products but not eggs, meat, fish and any other animal produce. He feared a fainting spell at the sight of the animals. But this exercise was mandatory for us in the exams, where we were marked on the sketches of the opened bodies. Vikram suggested he will memorize the required diagrams and reproduce them on paper. He was given the exemption—unfair because he would come prepared with the answer while others had to draw from the visual on their table.

'Do any Radha Soami followers become doctors,' I asked Vikram. 'Good question,' he said. 'I am sure they do. The ones with a robust constitution.'

Forced to Pick Science. Did I Lose a Decade of My Life?
February 20, 1986

I urged, begged, cajoled and cried but to no avail. My father was adamant I pick science and not commerce and economics in class eleven.

Everyone studied the same subjects till the tenth but had to choose their streams in senior school. Engineering or medicine were seen as safe choices at the time and thus the bias towards opting for science in high school. Even though my high grades reflected otherwise, I had neither an interest nor an understanding of anything science. My father—a dominant figure—would not hear of any of it. He had ambitions of a son eventually graduating from the famed IIT.

I would struggle with science in class eleven and twelve and had to rely on additional tuitions and rote learning to finish a credible ninth in school (down from first in class and second in school overall in class ten). It got worse—my grades were good enough to secure admission to the Delhi College of Engineering, a top ten college in the country. They offered me a seat, and I was forced to accept it, under protest. I would sink to the bottom of my class there.

I would spend a decade studying or working in science and technology. A misfit psychologically and in ability, it further influenced personal choices I would later regret. I would unshackle myself eventually and tried rebuilding in areas of my interest, but the foundations had weakened.

Life became a series of experiments—personal and professional—making it a journey without a pattern or a plan. I would stay angry with my father for as long as he was alive, always in a tussle to break free from him and yet staying yoked together. Only after his passing did I find myself on a different vantage point, offering me views I had never visualized. A new understanding dawned upon me: no decade or decades were lost. On the contrary, even if by accident, I discovered a meaning of existence lost on my peers. Their lives were spent building a single edifice, whereas mine has been about dotting my landscape with cabins—each a repository of stories. On hindsight, I will not exchange my village for the cities my classmates built. Because I am at peace here. With myself. And with my father.

A Primer on Preparing for Class Ten Boards. Includes Looking at Girls.

The ICSE boards are not easy to prepare for. Not just for the content, but for the schedule.

Over the course of ten working days, we had to appear for eleven written exams and three laboratory practicals for physics, chemistry and biology. We would have two exams on one day, one on the next and so on. We only got a few hours between each paper to revise the course. All other boards would stretch the same number of exams over weeks.

For three months leading up to the boards, I followed a schedule, any deviation not an option. Wake up at four, study till six, take a milk break, loiter a bit and be back at the desk at seven. Two more hours before breakfast, followed by another hour. Take a siesta for two hours. Wake up to the fun part.

Around one, I would drive out and pick up Anish and Manav—they stayed in neighbouring Hauz Khas. I stayed in Asian Games Village, built to accommodate athletes participating in the 1982 edition in New Delhi. These apartments were then sold off—most to the Government owned public sector corporations and a few to the private sector. My father got one allotted in the former category.

We would then drive around for about forty-five minutes, looking at girls getting off their school buses. Particularly those from all-girls schools: Mater Dei, Carmel, Loreto and CJM. We just drove past them, slowly, judging them, falling in love for the afternoon. That's it.

We did not make catcalls, nor did we hoot or honk. We did not even try to strike up conversations. In fact, the girls never realized they had secret admirers on the prowl.

Having got our doses of dopamine, we headed back home to the grind. Have lunch, study two hours, take a break, study more, drink milk, step out in the neighbourhood to meet friends for a bit, come back to study an hour, have dinner and then be at my desk till midnight. Lights out till the alarm went off at four.

Studying entailed writing. Everything. Multiple times over. It was vital to memorise the course material so revisions just before the exams were breezier. I tested myself, improving scores each time I did. By the time the boards came around, I had 91 per cent in my head and could refresh in the few hours available between papers. Where did this number come from? That's how much I would go on to score overall.

The hard work paid off when the results came out.

The girls never got to know of the three boys they motivated to be at their academic best.

The girl-spotting would go a bit too far. We continued our afternoon rituals even after the boards since we were free in the mind. I was infatuated with a neighbour from Carmel Convent and I knew the precise time she would return from school. I left home daily to cross her when she got off her bus at the gates of Asian Games Village where we lived. I spotted her as usual and started waving to her while driving—we were acquainted so she waved back. I did not notice the aghast expression on her face even though my eyes were on her—she saw me drive my grandfather's car into the entrance gates. The car and the gate were ruined but I survived with only a slight bruise on my chest. The incident became a joke in the neighbourhood.

Of course, everyone was upset at home. But the board results came out within days of the accident and I topped the school. Everything was forgiven and forgotten. I never got to date the girl.

Half Monty to Impress CJM Girls
March 24, 1986

'You are not going to impress me with your shirt off, you little boy!'

Mrs Kak cut Pritash Mathur to size with these words, making the giant of a boy feel like a midget. Teachers have an uncanny sense of timing and she walked in just when a bunch of 10-E boys were at the windows, monkeying with their shirts off. To impress CJM girls across the wall. Pritash attracted attention of the teacher first with his frame in a heightened state of animation. He stood topless, pink with embarrassment, speechless while others scurried to put their shirts on before the gaze fell on them.

The girls had been waving back with equal enthusiasm but had the sense of keeping their shirts on. They might have given an impression of liking the boys but were likely feeling excited as in a zoo, try to figure how to get peanuts across to the simians.

We were in a merry mood to mark the end of the boards but would either need to curb our enthusiasm or move to another location where a Mrs Kak would not appear.

Rumble in the Jungle
March 28, 1986

Never challenge Rohit Valia if you want unadulterated soup. Or if you do not want to scare wild animals.

The post-boards celebrations took a hundred of us to the Jim Corbett National Park on a school trip; we stayed in Dhikala, a camp deep inside the forest. We bunked in dormitories and were warned not to step out at night lest any wild animals sniff us out for a family meal.

We had to line up for food at appointed hours. On the first night, Rohit took soup in his cup, tasted it, made a face, poured the rest back in the cauldron and walked away before the bewildered Mr Walter could react. Why did he do this? Because Bobby Singh dared him to. Did he get soup at all? Of course not. He could not go back but the antic was worth missing out on.

The same night, Rohit let out a blood-curdling scream after lights went out in the camp. The stillness and the silence of the dark was broken and I am sure I heard wings fluttering—birds woken from their slumber. Only Rohit knew how to do this—it originated in the pit of his stomach, rising to the throat, where it finds the perfect amplifiers to reach the skies and then bounce back. Why did he do this? Because Bobby dared him to. I wonder if he put the fear of wild boys from Columba's into predators of the jungle, keeping them at bay during our stay? Incidentally, he would let this cry out twice in Chanakya cinema when we were in college; he timed it perfectly. Once when a woman is murdered on screen and another when a girl met a boy for the first time in a romantic movie. You don't want to know what happened when he screamed.

We were taken on a safari the following morning, dozens of us squeezed atop three elephants. The mahouts suddenly brought the animals to a halt, signalling we make no sound. They had spotted a male tusker in musth—being sighted by him would have spelt trouble in all caps! They discreetly turned the elephants around, tiptoeing away before urging the animals to trot. Yes, we were running away. The landscape was uneven and undulating and we had to go down and then up deep nallahs (dry stream beds) and it fascinating how the large animals navigated the landscape. We were swaying in the howdah all the way through—sure that we would tip over. We did not. And lived to tell the tale. It may have seemed like a harmless adventure, but the warden emphasised repeatedly on our good fortune. I wonder if Rohit's scream would have the driven the tusker away.

There was a couple from New Zealand who were camping in Dhikala—two adults barely squeezed into a pup tent. They became the talk of our group with boys imagining what was happening in the tent at night, salivating at the prospect of taking the man's place.

This was my first visit to Corbett, missing out a chance to come earlier on a school trip in class seven. My mother started bawling on the morning of departure—said she won't be able to bear my being away. For three days! She promised to take me to a movie if I agreed not to go. I was cornered and stayed put. The departure got delayed by half an hour because they were waiting for me. When I was told of this later and of all the fun others had, I swore never to let my mother emotionally blackmail me again.

Talking Poverty on Way Back from Corbett
March 31, 1986

Put a hundred boys in two buses and they could bring a house—or the highway—down with their energy. And their decibels. Profanities, songs, small talk—it was a cacophony, with little regard to the presence of teachers and their families with little girls.

We took a break along sugarcane fields to relieve ourselves. Most eyes followed Mr and Mrs Wintle as they sought privacy amidst the tall growth. No one could see anything after the lady lowered herself, but they kept staring as if the plants would part to give us a view. Perverts, each of us.

Things did sober up as darkness fell. Some dozed off, a few put their Walkman on, those who could read under dim lights in moving vehicles took their books out. I was making small talk with ace swimmer Ravi Bhalla when he said something I have never forgotten.

'The neighbourhood we live in, if some coins drop on the street, the sound brings a crowd together to look at the money. Because everyone is so poor,' he said.

We were not rich by any stretch of the imagination; my father was on a modest Government salary. But poverty was not talked about in such abject terms. It hit home deeper because one of my classmates was talking about it. He clearly came from lesser means than us, but we all felt at par because of the school we were in. That's why St. Columba's mattered.

Entered Class Eleven: We Are in Senior School
April 2, 1986

Call it the big migration. After six years in the Middle School, we moved to the Senior School. It would be the last two years of our time in St. Columba's. A critical time, because our performance would now shape a future we still could not anticipate.

I would move from section D to C—to study English, Physics, Chemistry, Mathematics and Computers. Electronics was optional; I dropped it without a thought. The science syllabus was too much for me to add to it. Mr Peter Rocha was appointed our class teacher.

Sadly, several of our brilliant and longest serving teachers left school at the same time. Including Mrs M. Kak (history), scout master Mr C. Innis, Ms N. Khosla (English), Mr R.R. Sawoo (swimming coach), Ms B. Vander Holt (elocution), and Mr and Mrs Wintle. Mr Reginald Rocha too, the one who slapped me on the street for shooting him with a water pistol. The biggest loss was of Br Barry and Mr Pokhriyal, exceptional mathematics teachers, one of whom would have taught us in Senior School.

I Leave Columba's for DPS
April 1986

Ever played the game of musical chairs? Three of us did, the chairs spread across two schools.

I decided to move to the R.K. Puram branch of Delhi Public School, commonly called DPS or DPS RKP. Why did I shift? The school had an ability section for the brightest, paying special attention to prepare them for admission to the Indian Institute of Technology or IIT. That's how they sent a disproportionate number to what was regarded as the MIT of India—in reputation at least, if not in teaching and research standards. It gave the school bragging rights, further attracting the best of teachers and students.

That's how I could make a case to be allowed to move. My father wanted nothing more than to see me in IIT one day and so agreed readily. My mother was disappointed of course; she had wanted her son to be in St. Columba's. If anyone thought I had become besotted by science suddenly, they were mistaken; it was just a pretext to seek out the company of girls!

Rohit Valia and Anish Tawakley moved too—they genuinely wanted to get into IIT. Mr Lugani, the principal, promptly admitted us; three of the brightest Columbans shunning their school for DPS was something to be smug about. Seats were expanded to accommodate us. Columba's was abuzz about the 'defectors' as if we had broken through the Iron Curtain, the difference being we moved from 'west' to the 'east.' It was like downgrading ourselves socially.

We made news. And then we made bigger news. Within five days, all three of us were back, each for our own reasons. DPS was not what I had expected. I felt a misfit in a class of nerds on the first day itself. They had nothing to talk about beyond science and mathematics. Each of them borrowed technical books from the library, I borrowed a pictorial biography of Hollywood star Richard Burton. The grime got to me and I was not taken in by any of the girls. I wanted to go back to Columba's, my home, my comfort zone.

Anish trotted back in a show of allegiance to his best friend. Rohit found DPS a zoo and was aghast to see there were no desks. At Columba's we had proper ones with storage; DPS had a chair with a side flap to write on.

We walked into our classrooms in St. Columba's as if nothing had happened, but Mr Rocha told us to report to the principal before we could take a seat. Br Pinto would not take us back initially. He had scratched our names off the rolls. 'But we never left school,' we protested. 'Of course you did, even if you did not inform us officially,' he said. But he was big Brother to us and had to take us back. But there was a complication: we were in section C, the ability one. Our vacant seats were given to "lesser mortals" who moved from B to C. They could not be sent back, so seats were added for us.

Wait—there is more. After a few days, something put Rohit off when we were discussing Macbeth. He did not want anything more to do with the English teacher. He could not wish her away, so he went back to DPS. His seat had been given away by then—but the principal still took him in.

Rumours floated about Mr Lugani swearing never to admit any Columbans in the future.

And that is how the game of musical chairs played out during the early weeks of class eleven.

P.S. I wonder if I can claim to be an alumnus of DPS for the five days spent there and Air Force Bal Bharti School for kindergarten, the grade I repeated in Columba's?

Br Pinto Ko Gussa Kyon Aata Hai?

Why does Br Pinto get angry? For that matter, other Brothers and teachers too. Here is a list of 'crimes' you could commit to attract their ire—in no particular order of severity. Includes why you would get thrashed even without just cause.

- Talking and creating ruckus during classes.
- Be seen in corridors without reason.
- Eating in class.
- Any pranks.
- Inattentive in class.
- Messing in the laboratory.
- Masturbating under the desk.
- Unkempt school uniform. Includes unpolished shoes, unironed and unclean clothes, missing tie or belt, tie with improper knot, not wearing uniform prescribed in summers and winters, wrong material or shades of fabric used.

- Flying missiles.
- Being spotted in a cinema, market or any other place during school hours.
- Fighting.
- Smoking a cigarette.
- Smoking a pen or pencil.
- Possessing cigarettes.
- Graffiti on walls.
- Failing in a subject.
- Falling short of hundred by five marks or under.
- Homework not done.
- Forgetting to carry required textbooks and notebooks.
- Textbooks not covered properly with brown paper.
- Roller-skating in school.
- Firing a slingshot or any other weapons.
- Flinging chalk and cleaning dusters.
- Playing video games.
- Reading *Mastram*, the popular porn magazine of the day.
- For calling Nanak Mehta a chaiwala (tea seller); Gautam Hazarika got slapped for it.
- Forging signatures of parents in school diary or test papers.
- Bad hormone day.

- Childhood trauma—not heard of that time but now talked about.
- Any day a teacher would lose their patience.

Have Charlie, Will Swing

When we were studying reasons behind the first world war, one was the arms buildup—the generals twitching to use them because the arsenal had not been assembled to shoot birds on holiday after all. Teachers had their own weapons—wooden ruler, cane, leg of a chair and the good old hands besides others. They could not just see them lying around—their use could be justified only if they built an anger within. Thus, they would get upset over the most specious of reasons to lash out!

Will Corporal Punishment Work Today?

Unlikely. Because societal norms have changed, according to teachers from times past.

Striking children physically to punish or discipline was seen as normal, both in school and at home. But pampering became a key tenet of parenting from the turn of the century. Not only did parents desist from hitting children but they seem to tolerate insolence and give in to demands to show their love. Also to rid of guilt for not having enough time for their children given their hectic professional and social lives.

It would thus be unnatural for schools to inflict corporal punishment as children are neither used to it nor would it be acceptable. If you want to meet Charlie, you might have to visit a retirement home or a museum. Or navigate the corridors of St. Columba's at night with the Ghostbusters.

Let There be Darkness
April 8, 1986

Was there going be an audition for *The Four Musicians of Bremen?* We entered class find Mahesh Srinivasan standing on a desk, Sanjeev Bawa on his shoulders reaching for the ceiling. They were fiddling with the starter of the tube lights. 'Don't remove them, just loosen them slightly so they don't come on.' It would thus take longer to diagnose the problem.

Just in time before Mrs Kapoor, the stand-in Physics teacher while Mrs Trisal was on maternity leave, walked in. The room was too dark to teach, the electricians not readily available. She tried to write on the board, managing with any light coming through the windows. Only to be continually interrupted by students complaining it was too dim to take notes.

The following day was no more productive. The blackboard was in two parts and you pulled strings to bring one down and send the other up. Someone cut the string, leaving only limited area to write as both boards were resting one behind the other. With complex equations and diagrams to be drawn and shown together, the teacher had to compress everything in the space available. Backbenchers kept heckling because they could not read the 'scribbles' given the distance.

Only Rajeev Barua was not amused; he was on mission to make it to the best universities and our idiotic behaviour was not helping his cause. Knowing how he got agitated only added to our entertainment.

In all this, I wanted to walk out and enrol in section D to study economics. I should have.

Education at Rs 100 a Month

We were beneficiaries of one of the finest educational institutions not just in India, but in the world. Even after adjusting for inflation and cost of living, the monthly tuition fee was Rs 75, the optional bus service costing another twenty-five. A total of Rs 100. That's it.

Corporatisation of education has resulted in astronomical fee structures. They may be preparing students well for any careers they choose, but few, if any, have attained the status of schools like St. Columba's. Because it takes more than money to build fine institutions.

St. Columba's could not have attained the status it did without its teachers. They were some of the brightest minds out there who would have readily been accepted in many other professions offering significantly higher remuneration and perks.

'If teachers are what they wanted to be, other schools would have readily paid them more than what they earned in St. Columba's,' Mr Peter Rocha once told me. They might have earned higher if the fee was increased, but the school did not

want to burden anyone even if it meant their own teachers and management made sacrifices.

But they chose to work in St. Columba's. Because they knew that if they did not, no one else of their calibre would. The values they stood for, and imbibed in us, made us who we are. They were selflessness personified.

While one can give back to the school in many ways, one can never do enough to compensate for what the school gave us. After all, you cannot measure or put a price tag to commitment, quality and sincerity.

Even after adjusting for all indices economists come up with, where can you 'buy' education' for Rs 100 today?

We Lose a Classmate to Underage Driving
April 21, 1986

We reached school to sobering news. Yajuvendra Anand had passed away over the weekend.

We had been together since kindergarten, and I could not help but feel terrible about someone I had grown up with. He was not a friend. On the contrary I feared him; in some ways I despised him. I almost choked while swimming in Delhi Gymkhana Club once because Yajuvendra's idea of a prank was forcing my head under water. I was no match for his strength and size but managed to break free in time.

But in his passing, I felt someone close had gone away. After all, we had been together for eleven years. He lost his life to sheer negligence. He was riding a bike; his parents allowed him on the condition he sit behind the driver. Once away from home, he forced the driver to let him take the front seat. The bike skid and fell near Moolchand Hospital. With no visible injury, he dusted himself and swore the driver to secrecy lest he be scolded at home.

He went home, had dinner and went to bed. Never to wake up again. His lung had got punctured in the accident.

Underage driving is rampant in India. I have been guilty of it too. I started driving at fourteen. My parents never allowed me to ride a bike though. It upset me when I was a college student but am glad they drew a thick line on this one.

'You Won't Even Know Where the Hole Is'
May 1, 1986

Anish and I were discussing women and their anatomy as if we were God's appointed lover boys to them. Krishna Wahi was listening in, seemingly least interested, before our talk got to him.

'The first time you are with a woman, you will not be able to find the hole,' he said. And moved to the back of the bus so he wouldn't have to listen to 'amateurs' anymore. He was a thick set guy, with the demeanor and body hair of a fully grown man. Sounding experienced like one too, not a sixteen-year-old. We looked at each other, stifling our giggles, as if privy to a secret: he has done 'it.'

We had been happy in our virgin fantasies, but doubts crept in: will we be able to navigate our way through when we are finally with a woman? Maybe he should give us some lessons if he was so cocksure of himself.

The Smartest Class in School is Suspended!
May 7, 1986

Our section C represented the academic royalty. Those with the highest grades in tenth had the first option to choose subjects, a majority going for those offered in C.

It resulted in a cocky lot coming together from all the five sections in tenth. The mix proved potent. We just could not be disciplined, reserving our worst behaviour for Mrs J. Trisal who taught physics and Mrs D'Souza, the new mathematics teacher. What did we do?

Talk incessantly during lectures. Pass food around. Stomp our feet rapidly in sync like an army company. Interject with inane questions. Point to a leaky bladder, seeking permission to step out. Sabotage tube lights. Hide the duster, requiring the teacher to wipe the blackboard with her saree or a piece of thermocol (polystyrene used for packing). Send paper missiles flying around. Oranges too. One struck the wall when Probir Rao missed catching it, leaving a mark for at least the two years while we were there. Our chests would swell with pride each time our eyes fell on it as if it were a martyr's memorial.

The matter finally reached Br Pinto who had no choice but to suspend us. Two days before school closed for the summers. We ran out in jubilation. Our class would be the envy of other sections!

I Was First in School. Then Dropped to Second.
July 7, 1986

It would be the lowest day of my thirteen years in St. Columba's School.

The class ten board results had come out in May—not only had I topped my section, but the school. I checked and re-checked to be sure. I could not believe it. No one else could either.

The summer holidays were spent over the moon. My name would go up on the board where all school toppers were listed. And stay there for posterity.

But things came crashing down the moment the school re-opened. The final certificates with board results came out—and I was pushed down to second. Ashish Mohan was the topper. What happened? Did he submit his papers for re-evaluation? Must have; how else would his scores improve?

There was nothing I could do about it. His name went up on the board. My photo was published in the school magazine though for coming second. I would not have felt bad had I not topped when results were initially declared; but to drop in rank like this was a bitter pill to swallow for a sixteen-year-old.

No matter how philosophical I am about it, the disappointment rankles me to this day. Every wound in my life has healed, this refuses to.

Ordeal Under Sun and Rain for Walking Out of Class

July 15, 1986

Fifty boys standing in the sun for three hours. The humid ordeal made worse by the ban on water and toilet. Only for it start raining too—weather can be fickle during the monsoon months.

But isn't that what class 11-D wanted? Why else would they walk out of Mrs Sharma's maths class collectively? The boys knew there would be repercussions, but did not expect Br Pinto to send them out like this.

It was a day for everyone to be upset. Mrs Sharma and Br Pinto as expected to be. The boys for the nature of the punishment; caning would have been gentler. Even Charlie threw a tantrum—for being denied the bounty of fifty backsides to whip!

The Games We Played During the Break

Boys needed to sweat it out. At every opportunity. Hundreds of us were seen playing during the break, games unique to us.

Frisbee

Break time meant a game of frisbee. With no rules.

Two teams would form by themselves. Any number could join in, their endeavour to get the frisbee into goals used for both football and hockey. The game would last the entire duration of the break. Anyone could join and leave either team at any stage. You just kept playing till the bell rang.

How would one distinguish team members? If you were moving left to right, you were on one team; if moving right to left, then the opposing one. Loyalties could switch anytime. The intent was to release pent-up energies, work up a sweat and show a bit of masculine swagger.

Did I mention the obstacles? They came in the form of hundreds of boys just loitering in the field. It did not deter the players, adept as they were in 'dribbling' through the crowd. No apologies were offered for knocking anyone's tiffin. It was in our interest to watch out for a stocky guy running in our direction, eyes only on the frisbee.

Football on the Basketball Court

A version of football was played on the concrete basketball courts during the break; the ball was a piece of stone you kicked around. The free-for-all approach meant anyone could join and drop out when they felt like.

This game did more to damage our black leather shoes than anything else. Tears and holes could appear anytime, requiring a visit to the cobbler after we had been scolded at home. Everything cost hard-earned money. If you tripped and tore your trousers and got a bloody gash, then you were recommended to pray for leniency all the way home.

Hand Cricket

A game for the lesser agile. Played with a tennis or ping pong ball. The bat was your palm or a book, the wickets would be any hedges and the pitch no longer than four yards. Teams could be just one player or more. You played an equal number of deliveries, runs scored deciding the winner. Most games were left unfinished when Walter rang the bell to mark the end of the break.

Pocket Ping Pong a.k.a. Pocket Billiards

This is for the lazy sportsman. Put your hands in your trouser pockets and jostle with any spherical and cylindrical objects you could feel between the legs. At least one of them would undergo varying changes in length and firmness, so tight legwear is avoidable for best performance.

Everyone thought no one would notice us playing, but one look and we would know if the hands in the pockets were there for the comfort or for the games.

It's a single player game, no one wins or loses, but pleasure is guaranteed. And as is obvious, it is a game only for boys to play.

I Am An 'Out-Standing' Singer
July 23, 1986

'You have an outstanding voice. You may now stand outside.'

That's how Siddhartha Mukherjee silenced my singing career. He was putting together a group song in Bengali, and I signed up for the auditions; I don't know where I developed the confidence or rather the audacity to. During the practice session, Siddhartha heard jarring notes—figured mine was standing out from the rest and dismissed me.

I never attempted to sing in public again. When I did croon, it was for private audiences who loved me too much to not just tolerate me, but also say I am a good singer.

Siddhartha Mukherjee, one year my junior, would be awarded the coveted Sword of Honour for his all-round capabilities in the final year of school. He went on to win the Pulitzer for his book, The Emperor of All Maladies: A Biography of Cancer. I suppose geniuses like him know what they are doing when making music too.

The Squirrel Attending Classes from Inside Mr Rocha's Shirt
July 28, 1986

Mr Peter Rocha had something big and long inside his shirt. Shirt, not trousers. Turned out to be a squirrel. Rescued, or kidnapped, from the school field. For the next many weeks, the squirrel would be with him—moving in and out of his shirt, sitting on his shoulder, running down his arm but never leaving his being. Mr Rocha would stay focused on the lectures as if there was nothing unnatural about a resident squirrel.

The school made another exception for him: admitted his daughter to kindergarten. Of course, she would be gone long before she got to an age where any of the classmates would ask her out. I can't imagine what it would have been like if she had been schooled throughout in Columba's—the only girl amongst 3,000 boys.

Colgate Inspired Ad for Contraceptive
August 4, 1986

> 'Hum savere uthte hain
> Sabse pehle lete hain
> Colgate ka chotta packet.
>
> Kholo, Dabao
> Brush pe lagao
> Colgate ka chotta packet.
>
> Mod ke rakho
> Phir kaam mein lao
> Idhar lao, Idhar lao
> Mujhe bhi do idhar lao.
>
> Colgate dental cream … ab chote packet mein
> Jyada chale, khub chale.'

The above television advertisement for a small tube of Colgate toothpaste had the country humming—but Amlan

Bhattacharya chose to tweak it just a little bit. And could not resist from humming it all day:

> 'Hum savere uthte hain
> Sabse pehle lete hain
> Nirodh ka chotta packet.
>
> Kholo, Dabao
> L*** pe lagao
> Nirodh ka chotta packet.
>
> Mod ke rakho
> Phir kaam mein lao
> Idhar lao, Idhar lao
> Mujhe bhi do idhar lao.
>
> Nirodh **** **** … ab chote packet mein
> Jyada chale, khub chale.'

Nirodh was a condom distributed for free by the Government or sold at a fraction of the cost of other brands at pharmacies. Its advertising was ubiquitous since the Government wanted to check population rise. For a long time, it was to condoms what Xerox was to photocopy.

Amlan had a propensity for getting into trouble, but few could match his sense of humour!

Dropping a Year's Pocket Money in the Poor Fund Box
August 18, 1986

Rana Nanda dropped Rs 1,000 in the Poor Fund box. It was not a mistake. He did not steal the money. He always finished first or second in class.

He just did it—no fuss, no glory.

Many of us received less than that as pocket money in a year. That would have been enough to feed the class a Nirula's burger and a cola each. Or buy 2,000 patties, 1,000 chole bhature, a professional cricket kit, 500 front rows tickets at Chanakya cinema, 200 *Debonair* porn magazines.

It would have fed a poor family for weeks. Or sent two of their children to school for a year.

No Fear of a Nuclear Meltdown
August 28, 1986

Everyone seems to love the prospect of a nuclear war. It gives politicians a campaign to garner votes, capitalists to profit from arms trade and filmmakers to win accolades. Thus, the success of the made-for-television film, *The Day After*, directed by Nicholas Meyer. Released in 1983 at the time of renewed Cold War tensions between the Western and Soviet Union blocs, it captivated audiences with haunting imagery of the aftermath of nuclear attacks on America.

A video of the film reached the school three years after its initial release. It was the year when Russian and American leaders Mikhail Gorbachev and Ronald Reagen initiated talks to pare back on their nuclear arsenals and build safeguards against nuclear conflicts. The negotiations ended with mixed results but would turn out to be a precursor of political liberalisation of communist Europe.

The film didn't really move any of us. We could not be bothered with the scaremongering of the Cold War. We had a meaningless discussion post the screening; Mr Rocha realized he must get different kinds of films to analyse.

The Loud(est) Fart by Mohnish Mohan
August 29, 1986

We experienced deathly silence the day before. And the loudest fart possible the day after.

The screening of *The Day After* was an exercise in near-silence. The movie itself had minimal dialogues and background sounds. We were quiet watching it, pretending to understand the gravity of the scenarios being depicted but bored to hell, in reality.

In contrast, the morning after started with a long, loud sound—who had let it rip so badly? It was a whoopie cushion Mohnish Mohan had picked during the family holiday to New York. He placed it under Sarthak just when he was lowering himself on his chair. Fortunately, it only simulated the sound and not the stink of a fart.

The class burst into spontaneous laughter but Mr Rocha was not amused in the least. He quietly walked to Sarthak's desk, picked the object of disruption and resumed the analysis of *Lord of the Flies*. He did not speak a word about the incident, and all of us (sensibly) got the cue and heard him out in pin drop silence.

The toy was never returned.

When Columban 'Girls' Outperformed Shahrukh Khan's Girl
September 7, 1986

'Boy in Mini Skirt Strangles Another Boy in Mini Skirt'

If Rohit Srivastava had not been restrained, the country would have woken up to this newspaper headline on Sunday. Youth Quake by Bang Club, the inter-school multi-disciplinary competition was on and all those who could get hold of scarce tickets would be in attendance at the Siri Fort Auditorium. Rohit and Varun Pawha were a part of the theatre cast—the former as the blond Bondie, and the latter the brunette Bondie. Their costumes included wigs, oranges for breasts and mini-skirts borrowed from sisters of schoolmates.

'Shave your legs to add a touch of authenticity,' Rohit was told. He thought, 'Good idea,' and got down to it. After cleaning one leg, he felt there was too much hair—something was amiss and he felt the need to check if he was doing it correctly. He went backstage, one leg hairy, the other shiny and smooth. The troupe cracked up at the sight, congratulating themselves for pulling the prank off. Those present would recount how Rohit let out every expletive ever uttered and then some original ones too. He could have punched or even choked Varun and the others had stronger arms not restrained him.

We would go on to win the theatre segment and the overall trophy too. The victory was sweeter because we also beat Modern School Vasant Vihar. They had Gauri Khan in the lead and the play was directed by our famous alumnus, Shahrukh Khan. The two would get married five years later and Shahrukh would move from Bang Club to be amongst the biggest stars Bollywood has ever seen. But on that day, our 'girls' beat his!

Sex Education Derailed by Dirty Talk
September 19, 1986

You could say the affair did not last long. Br Deasy's efforts to impart sex education classes and help us understand women better through letters came a cropper.

In the first phase, he explained through slideshows how the two genders differ physically, in their psychological make-up, in their approach to intimacy and love and how the maturity curves are not in sync. As a further experiment, our Brother got a Sister from CJM to agree to an exchange of letters with their class eleven girls. Both sides could ask anything and sign off with a code name known only to the sender.

The first round passed smoothly. We asked simple questions about their likes and dislikes, any hobbies they pursue, what appeals to them in boys. The girls replied, asking similar questions, signing off with cryptic names themselves. In the next round, some clown decided to check if hormones were raging on the other side too—and went onto write a graphic description of his anatomy and about things he does to himself under the sheets at night. The reply came, no less graphic. Yes, the girl was on fire too!

The problem was Br Deasy went through the reply in a breach of confidentiality. He read bits out loud, asking code name Superman 2000 to stand up. No one did. No problem. Letters were distributed and all but Gaurav Narula got theirs. His Superman avatar stared silently, face ashen, mumbling apologies when he found his voice.

The worst did not happen—there was no corporal punishment, no moral lectures, no walk to the principal office. But the program was suspended, much to our disgust. We will never know which girls wrote to us.

If we were in a residential school, I am sure a bunch of us would have ambushed him, covered him with a blanket and beaten him till every drop of testosterone was squeezed out of him.

Shane Warne Denies Rammohan a Spot in Australia's Cricket Team

September 27, 1986

'The Australian cricket team does not have an off spinner. I will move there and will be granted citizenship instantly because they will want me to play for their country.'

Thus spoke Rammohan Subramanium during a practice session. Bowling left arm and on the school team, he made the above declaration with the supreme confidence of one who has it all figured. In the moment, I was both in awe and envy of him. Australia? Wow!

Another Australian, the same age as our batch, would make his debut as a leg-spinner for his national team before we graduated from university and would hold the world record for test wickets for a long while. There was thus no room for the services of another spin bowler. Rammohan had to go back to the drawing board to chart an alternate course for his life. All because of a guy named Shane Warne.

When the Class Took It a Bit Too Far
October 14, 1986

Mr Thomas finally had a nervous breakdown. The ragging by class 11-E got the better of him.

The economics teacher had to tolerate heckling, cat calls and all possible forms of sound effects. He was used for target practice; peanuts and any other object capable of flying through air would be released in his direction whenever he had his back to the class. Boys would squirt ink from fountain pens on his back while we walked the aisles delivering his lecture; he would see the stains only when back home unless someone in the staff room pointed it out earlier.

He finally lost it, huffing off to the principal, rambling incoherently, choking over tears. Br Noronha came down to reprimand the class, delivering a lecture on decency and respect. He could not inflict any harsher punishment since culprits could not be identified. It still had the desired effect though; the class behaved themselves better with Mr Thomas.

Not that the boys turned pious overnight; wonder which teacher bore the brunt of their teenage energies?

Know My Enemy
October 24, 1986

'Do any of you have an enemy,' asked Mr Peter Rocha. I was one of the three who raised their hands.

I don't know what the exercise was for—maybe to do with the dark themes of our prescribed English texts, *Lord of the Flies* and *The Tragedy of Macbeth*. More significantly, who was my enemy? Kaustav Mitra.

An altercation took place between Jatin Verma and I on the bus ride home when I was in seventh; Kaustav, sitting behind me, punched me in the right ear. He had no business to get involved.

I got off at my stop and went home with my head tilted, to comfort my ear against my shoulder. It had stopped hurting, but I had taken a dramatic licence to make a show of it. Not that anyone cared—even Anish and Manav, my friends and neighbours, ignored me.

I stretched the theatrics at home, upsetting my mom. She went with me to the bus stop the following morning and gave it off to Kaustav. It only made things worse, as I was ragged for days on end by other boys for being the 'cry-baby' and 'mamma's boy.'

I would hate Kaustav for putting me through this. We moved home within a year and my bus changed. I avoided eye contact with him in the future—but continued to despise him. So, when Mr. Rocha asked if anyone had an enemy, I raised my hand. For something that happened four years ago.

I bet Kaustav would have no memory of who I was within days of the incident in the bus. But I kept nursing a grudge. Pointlessly.

I did give the devil his due though. Kaustav was given his due admiration for excelling as Dorothy in *The Wiz;* yes, he had a face to pass off as gentle girl's even if he had a violent head above it. We sang along when he crooned 'We will, we will rock you' in the Talkatora Indoor Stadium. Only we modified the lyrics to 'We will, we will fuck you!'

Many years later, Kaustav would be staring down at me from a big screen—in a dedication to Br D'Souza at his memorial service. He had sent a video recording from the USA. The sight of my 'enemy' after thirty-seven years made me smile!

Three Sixes in a Lost Cause
October 28, 1986

For eleven years, I did not make the cut for any sports team even at the class level, forget playing for the school. I finally made it to the class 11-C cricket team. My debut was electric. I stepped on to the pitch, our team requiring fourteen runs off three balls. I hit three sixes—but we still lost. Why?

I was facing James Verghese, a left arm pace bowler, who opened for the school team. We had given up hopes of winning, so I faced him with nothing to lose and nothing to fear. First ball in and I hit a blinder of a shot. The ball landed on the roof of the Junior School building. My team was ecstatic. The next two also flew over the boundary, leaving marks on the building. That's eighteen runs scored!

Now comes the twist. Windowpanes of the Junior School stood in the line of fire of cricket balls, breaking at a financially unsustainable frequency. The likes of Vivek Razdan, our star cricketer, and other batsmen would wager to direct their shots at the glass to make it worse. The school management had to bring in a rule: any ball hitting the building directly would not count for any runs. That's when batsmen avoided hitting in that direction if they had to win matches.

That is why we lost despite my scoring the runs required. We protested, we howled, but rules were rules.

To this day, my classmates talk about my innings. Forgotten are the heroics of those who brought glory to their class or school. The unlikeliest of sportsperson is the one who etched his name in the anecdotal history of the school.

Don't Heckle Mukul to Stay Safe
October 31, 1986

Mukul Dev Kaushal almost beat me to pulp. All because Ajay Malhotra was smashing his bowling out of the ground. Because I made an umpiring error.

During practice the previous day, I was made umpire and I gave Ajay Malhotra out Leg Before Wicket—wrongly, because I did not know how to judge such calls. He was enraged and left for home in a huff and practiced like hell for the upcoming match against B section the following day.

Poor Mukul bore the brunt of his anger, leaving him demoralized, making him question his talent as a cricketer. And here I was, idiotically heckling Mukul from the sidelines. The two Ajays had him all riled up. He walked up to me in a huff after the innings got over, threatening to smash ever bone in my body. I still don't know what caused the restraint.

All because someone asked me to be the umpire.

Mukul had been class captain from middle school onwards. And boasted how he would get ace batsmen like Ajay Malhotra out in the first over, year on year. He went out on a low in senior school though—because he had a girlfriend by then, was in love and his focus shifted. His performance on the field suffered but it peaked elsewhere.

Cricketers like them were the stars of the day; everyone wanted to be seen with them. But the halo lasted only as long as school did, the grind of 'adulthood' overwhelming sporting and creative interests. Of course, some would still shine bright. Like Mukul Dev Kaushal from the big screens of Bollywood. And tragically, now as a star in the sky above.

High End Clothing Brands, Made to Order

Lee, Levis, Wrangler ... you name the brand of the jeans, and it could be yours. Custom stitched. Within an hour. For Rs 100.

There were scores of denim patterns and colours to choose from. Along with different designs for studs, patches, zippers—the fashion statement was yours to make. It was available exclusively at the many shops housed in Mohan Singh Place, an indoor market located within walking distance of school in Connaught Place. They had patches for popular brands from across the world even if the originals were not available in India and would affix one of your choice.

For those with a bigger budget, you could match the shoes with jeans: Nike, Puma, Adidas—most under Rs 400. Few would recognise these to be knock-offs of international brands; how many had seen the real stuff anyway to make a comparison in those days?

Of course, many a homegrown brand came up at the time: FU's (pronounced F Use), Wings, Stencil, Buffalo, Wanted, Numero Uno and Weekender to name a few. But the swagger still came from sporting global names, whether authentic or not.

My father's job required him to travel to the middle east almost every month. Even though I got my quota of authentic branded shoes and apparel from overseas, I would get jeans stitched additionally from Mohan Singh Place well into my university years.

Flunked for Not Writing His Name on the Paper

November 3, 1986

No matter how well he wrote his class tests, Mr Thomas would not give Varun Pawha more than five or six out of ten. Rajesh Bharadwaj, no brighter, managed over 90 per cent each time. 'Why am I being marked so harshly,' Varun would wonder even when he felt he had done a good job.

Varun copied Rajesh's paper the next time, finally managing a ten. Rajesh scored a nine! But there was a hitch. Varun forgot to write his name on the paper. When Mr Thomas called out to ask whose unsigned paper it was, Varun recognised his handwriting and claimed the ten marks.

I am deducting six marks for not writing your name, said Mr Thomas. Varun ended with a four, confirming he was a victim of teacher bullying.

Butter Would Not Melt in My Mouth
November 14, 1986

The past few weeks had felt like a holiday with the complete school putting together an expo, 'Rediscovering India.' Br Pinto conceived the event as an attempt to, as the title suggests, rediscover our own country, to embody the spirit of India.

Every classroom and the foyer were done up with a theme to progressively showcase the country from ancient times to the contemporary. Covering art, literature, culture, economy, technology and history. A village, complete with huts and costumed students, was fabricated in the Middle School grounds. Senior classes were briefed to project the future and we painted a grand picture; those were days of optimism with the young Prime Minister Rajiv Gandhi ushering in new ideas.

The weeklong event was attended by tens of thousands of students from schools across the city—they came by busloads daily. St. Columba's gave the appearance of being one big carnival, also giving us a chance to check out girls!

Of course, a lot of hard work went behind putting it all together. It also enabled us to get a free pass to leave school anytime for 'research.' I remember five of us going to the offices of *The Hindustan Times* newspaper to ask a journalist for some material. We wanted a photo of legendary singer Lata Mangeshkar, but he could not spare it. 'What if she dies tonight? We will need it for the newspaper,' he said. She would live on for another thirty-six years; millions of photographs of her would be accessible through the Internet by then.

I remember two things from that interaction. Someone had scribbled, 'Bak, Bak, Bakshi Bastard' on the journalist's door. His last name was Bakshi. He looked at me and remarked, 'Butter would not melt in your mouth.' I would not understand the meaning for years to come. When I did, I wondered what did he know that even I didn't? (*Don't look at me with suspicion, but he seemed to have read me correctly*)

I also got the chance to drive a Maruti Gypsy jeep during the event; owning one supposedly improved a man's oomph factor at the time. We needed a certain kind of fabric for the props urgently and Mohnish Mohan had some at home. He offered to let Anish Tawakley and me drive his Gypsy to his place to pick it. We argued who would drive and settled for one way each. It's a wonder no cops caught us—we were out in our school ties, clearly under the permissible age of eighteen. I had a licence though with the wrong date of birth—arranged for by an uncle from Ambala—but it was best no cop looked at it closely lest he catch my lie.

Scandalous News Report Triggers Scramble for Flying Career
November 24, 1986

Monday morning was abuzz with an article in a popular magazine. It talked about how pilots indulged in sexual liaisons with air hostesses in hotels during layovers in different cities.

Pilots occupy the highest position in the hierarchy of staff in an aeroplane and it is not easy for female flight attendants to check their advances. The men would knock on their doors at night, insisting on offering their company knowing they were unlikely to be turned away. At least that's the perception the journalist created.

It got boys in the school talking and excited. A career in flying seemed like a highly attractive option: high salaries, opportunities to fly around the world and enjoying the 'perks' mentioned in the magazine.

It was also the year when the country developed an infatuation towards Kitu Gidwani playing the lead in a television series, *Air Hostess*. Sexy and beautiful, the series took on a controversial topic: the moral character of women in the flying industry. Her boyfriend's mother is vehemently opposed to her son marrying an air hostess because one could not vouch for 'where all she had been.' The series was abruptly pulled off air after a few episodes and the nation would never know if the man would defy his mother to marry the woman he claimed to have loved.

Kenneth Pillai and his brother went on to become pilots. I am sure the media events of 1986 influenced their decision. Their father had been in the Merchant Navy, so the family was used to men being away for extended periods of time.

Mr Rosemeyer Ko Gussa Kyon Aata Hai?

Why does Mr Rosemeyer get angry? He did not need a reason to. It seems he was born angry with a mission to take down boys, innocent and guilty.

He had a hundred ways to interpret your conduct as offensive, punishing you in ever inventive ways. He had his own Charlie, its sheath being the back of his shirt. He had a peculiar technique to pull it out in the blink of eye when required; must have been inspired by cowboys of the wild west. He also used it to frequently scratch his back, proving he had the itch to be violent at every opportunity.

The worst punishment was reserved for those who took him for a fool. You may think he's looking out of the window during a test, an apt opportunity to cheat from your neighbour. He was looking at you though—in the reflection on the glass or the metal awning.

If you were lucky, you would be caned. It could get worse. He would rest a pencil through your fingers—each alternating above and below the pencil—and then strike your knuckles with a wooden ruler. Worst? We sat on covered wooden desks with the lid slanting towards the bench; he would raise the lid, put your head inside and then bring it down with a bang.

No necks broke, so no laws broken.

'Birthing' a Younger Brother to Enter His Girlfriend's School
December 1, 1986

'Sir, my younger brother is highly impressed with Laxman Public School and wants to move from St. Columba's to your school.'

The principal of LPS could not believe what Mukul Dev Kaushal was saying. It was flattering—a Columban holding his school in such high esteem! 'Send me his report cards and I will consider it,' replied the principal. 'By the way, what is that cylindrical object in the brown paper bag in your hand,' he enquired of Mukul.

'That's ketchup my mother asked me to pick on the way,' he replied. The conversation ended there.

What was Mukul doing in LPS with Badal? He wanted to meet his girlfriend and needed a pretext to be allowed into the compound. He conjured up an imaginary younger sibling and went in seeking admission. They could not locate his love interest though and came back disappointed.

The ketchup—seriously? Of course not. It was beer to enjoy with the girl; the two drank it by themselves anyway. No one asked for identification before selling alcohol in those parts even though rules required them to do so.

Br Pinto Sees Red When He Spots the Bisons
December 9, 1986

'When I see any of you Bisons, my sixth sense becomes hyperactive. I know trouble can erupt anytime like a volcano, that can billow smoke and ash without warning.'

Who were the Bisons? Mukul Dev Kaushal, Sanjay Sharma, Raja Kanwar, Mohnish Mohan and Vincent Hughes—literally the big boys of our batch. Br Pinto was addressing Raja and Sanjay, sharing his apprehension while also warning that they were being watched.

Not that the five could rattle Br Pinto. Experienced teachers like him must be used to wildlife on two legs year on year, adept at handling them. They had to be tolerated and yet loved despite whatever they did.

When Flowerpots and Pins Get Knocked Over During Bowling
December 19, 1986

Why would anyone pick up flowerpots in a hotel lobby and place them in the men's room? With Rahul Dass and Vipul Kapila, anything is possible.

A group of twenty odd had gone bowling to Qutab hotel when the two wandered off, collecting the pots and bringing them to the playing area. For no plausible reason other than to make the washrooms smell fresher. The authorities were certainly not amused; they sealed off the premises and called the cops. To book the boys for defacement of property.

Most terrified was Pavan Uttam—they had come in his car, packed like sardines. The driver was also detained. Pavan actually started crying, knowing he will have hell to pay at home. A plea of insanity was dismissed.

They were let off finally but only after they had restored the pots to their original positions and mopped the place of soil.

1986: Rajiv Gandhi's Honeymoon Over

In just over a year after being elected prime minister with a record majority, Rajiv Gandhi found himself stepping on a series of political mines. His coterie of advisers proved themselves to be poor navigators.

Under his watch the locks of the controversial Babri Masjid in Ayodhya were opened to satisfy the demands of Hindus. Through an Act of Parliament, he overturned a Supreme Court judgment guaranteeing maintenance to divorced Muslim women who could not support themselves; it would be known as the Shah Bano Case after the woman who sought justice for herself. Unfortunately, neither of these decisions appeased the intended communities, fuelling fires rather than dousing any. Riots in Kashmir, targeting Hindus in the state especially in the Anantnag district, only added to the young leader's concerns.

The government also contracted the Swedish arms company, Bofors, to supply over four hundred 155 mm Howitzer field guns. This deal would come back to bite Rajiv Gandhi, with his own defence minister V.P. Singh resigning the following year, citing corruption in defence deals. The Bofors scandal became a campaign cry in the 1989 general elections, the Congress ceding power to a coalition of parties who installed V.P. Singh as the prime minister.

On the cricket field, India and Australia were involved in only the second test to end in a tie. Shortly after India had made history, winning a test at Lord's against England for the first time, emerging series victors two games to nil.

Computer Games with Real Eggs
January 12, 1987

Mr Verma woke to find the windscreen of his red Maruti 800 car splattered with eggs. Anyone could have done it, but he was sure it was a bunch of Columbans. The matter reached the principal.

Br Pinto demanded the culprits step up, but no one did. The identities of the ten who did were an open secret, but no one ratted them out.

Not that it stopped there. The 'gang' went back repeatedly every night, smashing eggs on the car and the computer teacher's front door too. Their luck ran out on the fifth night: Mr Verma lay in wait and caught them in the act. Nine got away, but Rahul Dass got caught. The teacher dragged him home, locking him in the bathroom.

There was no mobile telephones but word got to Rahul's father and he showed up at the 'lock-up' in less than forty five minutes. Infamous for his temper, he grabbed Mr Verma by the collar and threatened to have him arrested for kidnapping his son. Ashish and Gautam, witness to this confrontation, swore Mr Verma wet his pants.

The situation diffused quickly enough. The 'outlaw' was released, everyone went their way and the eggs would stay in the frying pan, keeping their distance from any fire.

The school management was never told who the offenders were. We could never figure out the reason behind the provocation.

Good Education Just Needs Pen, Paper and a Blackboard

The duration of a school day was five and half hours, divided into eight periods and a break. Education aids were a blackboard and chalk, leaving hands and clothes dusty. We carried notebooks, ones made of paper, and pens. There was no air-conditioning, even fans worked erratically given the power cuts. And yet, we received education of the highest standards.

Because the focus was on basics. Teachers knew their respective subjects thoroughly and did not need to read out from notes or textbooks. We were made to use our hands, apply our minds. So, our brains developed, to be able to adapt to any demands and conditions in the future. If there were rapid advancements in science and technology in the coming decades, it was by harnessing the intellect of our generation.

Look at schools today. They keep students for seven to eight hours, the syllabus has far more subjects than we had, there are many more assignments to be submitted. Students are overwhelmed, with long hours in school followed by burdensome homework.

Not to forget the emphasis on frills like air-conditioned buildings and buses. Smartboards have replaced blackboards, notes are taken on tablets, there are screens all over. Smartphones, connected to the Internet, are being given to children at ever younger ages despite their negative effects having been proven. All in the name of preparing them to take on the world.

We did not need all of this and yet we can boast the sharpest and most creative of minds. Our capacity to work is limitless. If something must be done, it gets done. We don't need Charlie to whack us into action; we give weightage to work before demanding any balance with quality of life.

It is incredible how a group of capable teachers, committed to their cause, can shape generations of young people. Leading by standards they set for themselves, all it takes is chalk, pen and paper to impart the education needed to navigate life.

An Emotional Farewell Ends in Tragedy
January 25,1987

There was a scramble to find suits to wear during each of our senior years. In class eleven, when we would host a farewell for the twelfth graders and then a year later when we would be given a send-off. Most of us did not own suits of our own—and had to borrow from fathers, siblings and cousins. Of course they would be ill-fitting. I am sure Pavan Vaish eyed them as future customers—he would be the third generation of a family into custom tailoring, a career ordained at his birth.

It fell upon us eleventh graders to plan the party in the Junior School hall. The evening started on a docile note, students and teachers interacting with one another, not used to being with one another in a social setting. Then Br Pinto took the stage to deliver a tearjerker of a speech. If there were mobile cameras then, the recordings would have gone viral.

Dinner was served and staff was ushered in first. They must have known how evenings like these unravel; they quickly ate and left for home. There was no alcohol but you could sense a collective high building up. The first evidence of it took the form of something whizzing by my ear—upon inspection, it was a gulab jamun. The round, oily Indian sweet was released as a ball, disintegrating like comets in flight. Within minutes, the hall had become a battleground, all of us ducking lest any of these misguided flying objects strike us. We would have hell to pay when confronted by the owners of our suits had we gone back smeared with one.

Rotis, the hot breads, were added to the arsenal as frisbees. Then there was the fizz: covering the top of an aerated soft drink bottle with the thumb, shaking it vigorously, and then moving the thumb just a slight bit so the opening would let out a spray of bubbles and liquid. In all this, Mahesh was walking around with the countenance of the Buddha, dipping bread into a glass of water and biting into it. Yuck!

The party ended eventually, and we all went our ways. Some home, others to find another playground.

We woke the following morning to sombre news: Sameer Chandok, out late night with friends celebrating end of school, met with an accident and lost his life. We were told he had lost his father a few years ago, his mother and sister the only members left in the immediate family. The school would move future farewells from dinner to lunch.

Cardinal Sin: Do Not Make a Teacher Cry
February 10, 1987

Br Pinto looked into the staff room upon hearing the cries of someone. It was Mrs Sharma. One of the boys had spoken badly to her and she had broken down at the humiliation, walking out of the English lecture midway. You may expect teachers to develop a thick skin in this profession, but it can run only so deep.

'Out,' he ordered Sanjay Sikka sitting in the biology class. We heard the command, and then the slap in the adjoining room. We all looked outside. Sanjay recoiled backwards, Br Pinto stepped forward, continually slapping and kicking him. All the way to his office—you had to cross the entire length of the corridor and then a flight of steps to get there. Half the senior school witnessed it, each of us shuddering at the possibility of being thrashed like this. We had never seen anyone punished as severely as Sanjay was in twelve years.

Br Pinto would serve as principal till the end of the academic year, and I doubt whether anyone dared misbehave with a teacher to their face for as long as he was there.

Telephone Connection as Bribe to Pass Exam
March 16, 1987

Ashley Simon looked like he had seen a ghost. The commerce exam had just got over and he was sure to flunk it, holding back his promotion to twelfth. 'Don't worry, leave it to me,' assured Sanjay Sharma.

He approached Mr Bhatia, appealing to his charity in marking papers. 'I know Ashley, there are only so many grace marks I can give him,' said the tutor. 'I expect him to repeat the year.'

'May I call you in the evening to discuss this further,' asked Sanjay.

'I don't have a telephone line,' said Mr. Bhatia.

'Why don't you get one?'

'There is a wait of twenty years to get one.'

'Will you clear Ashley if I get you one?'

Sanjay had hit a sensitive spot. Mr. Bhatia was tempted. He looked Sanjay in the eye and believed he would deliver on the promise. Ashley was asked to be at Mr. Bhatia's residence the following Saturday where he reappeared for the exam, scoring the minimum passing marks.

Within a month, the world could call Mr Bhatia's family at home.

Despite liberalisation of the economy in the 1980s and the 1990s, the Government was the dog in the manger in the telecom sector. You could get landlines easily only in the twenty first century when private players got licences. Even when easily available, landlines did not need to become popular. State run departments continued to offer shoddy services, draining the exchequer when they had no reason to exist given the vast private networks in place.

I Flunk an Exam for the First Time
March 30, 1987

The final term exams results came out—and I flunked Physics. The first time for any subject in school. Quite a fall after finishing second in the boards just a few months prior.

I remember the drive back home after report cards had been collected, sitting on the front passenger seat of our Ambassador, my parents on the back seats. My father was chiding me for the disgrace, the neglect. In my mind, I was thinking this is what happens when my pleas to study commerce and economics were ignored, forcing me to pick science. I was amused despite the gravity of the situation, but I had to pretend to hang my head in shame.

The teacher had made an error in computing marks—and I did pass the subject after rectifications were made. But it was still a poor score. I have retained a copy of the report card, where the original thirty is still written in red.

The Son of an Accountant Scores a Zero in Accounts
March 30,1987

The son of a chartered accountant scored zero in the final exams. It became the joke of the year. How did KVK Vikram manage this feat?

Mr Xavier, called *Kancha* by all, had a policy of marking zero if any answer had two or more mistakes. Vikram made at least these many mistakes in each of the six answers and thus scored the minimum possible.

Parents were summoned to witness Vikram being shamed by the teacher. 'The future of your accountancy firm is in danger,' warned Mr Xavier. 'But you must be proud of your son in one aspect. The boy sitting next to him topped the class. Vikram could have easily copied from him, but he had the integrity not to.'

That did not console the seething, Vikram. He went on to score ninety-four in the boards the following year and was joint first all over India in the subject.

Br Pinto Leaves: End of an Era
April 1, 1987

We could call ourselves blessed and fortunate to have been in school when Br Pinto was the principal—but he could not have been there forever. He was meant for a higher calling, to serve people as dictated by his faith. An orator like few others we have heard, his parting words were published in the school magazine to be archived for posterity. An extract:

In his famous book 'The Prophet', Kahlil Gibran speaks of Al Mustafa getting ready to leave for his homeland after spending twelve years in the foreign city of Orphalese:

'But as he descended the hill a sadness came upon him and he thought in his heart: How shall I go in peace and without sorrow? Nay, not without a wound in the spirit shall I leave this city. Too

many fragments of the spirit have I scattered in these streets, and too many are the children of my longing that walk naked among these hills, and I cannot withdraw from them without a burden and an ache.' How true it all is!

I remember with what deep foreboding I stood at the school gate on my first day as Principal as hundreds of children were disgorged from cars and buses. Anxious parents fussed over their sons with last-minute instructions, and wary teachers eyed me suspiciously wondering what changes this new broom would bring. That daily routine at the gate was something I grew to enjoy, watching the innocence of little eyes, the cheery 'good mornings' the bubbling enthusiasm and energy of youth. Imagine my sense of gratification when I discovered that Edmund Rice, our Founder, also made it a point to welcome the children to school every morning!

It is said that a school is only as good as its staff. If St. Columba's has any standing today, it is mainly because of the many dedicated teachers that labour there. My greatest privilege was working with so many marvellous men and women who were such a support and source of strength.

'For this I bless you most:
You give much and know not that you give at all.'

People want to send their sons to St. Columba's because they say, 'Your school has discipline and you inculcate in your children a sense of values.' I rarely experienced any real difficulty with discipline. My memories of the Columban are happy ones. They often amazed me with the range of their abilities and their organisational skills. I rejoiced with them in their many successes and felt their disappointment when occasionally things went awry. I don't suppose things can be different when one becomes so involved in other people's lives.

'If in the twilight of memory we should meet once more, we shall speak again together and you shall sing to me a deeper song.'

Ashish Ahuja, a sixth grader, wrote a limerick for the departing principal:

> 'Our Principal is a bit hasty,
> He likes things which are tasty,
> He punishes boys who are disobedient
> But, actually, he's quite lenient,
> In fact, he's a sweet little pastry.'

Entered Class Twelve: The Countdown Begins

April 6, 1987

We are the seniormost students in St. Columba's School. The status also marks the beginning of the end. The end of our time in the school, the end of childhood, the end of togetherness of 250 of us. In less than a year, we will have left a place we entered aged five.

The school will feel different, Br Pinto no longer the principal, the charge now with Br C.D. Noronha. The set of teachers who taught us in eleventh will continue to in the twelfth too, since the boards covered the syllabus of both years.

Much Ado Over Cargo Pants
April 17, 1987

Final year of school did not give us a pass to be undisciplined, but some of us could not resist testing limits of tolerance of our teachers.

When Sanjay Sharma, Varun Pawha and Rajesh Bharadwaj decided to walk in wearing cargo pants, they were trying to make a fashion statement. Mr Chadha preferred to make one of his own.

As was fashionable at the time, out came Charlie, whipping both palms of Sanjay first and then Varun's. When it was Rajesh's turn, he switched into lawyer mode claiming he was entitled to a hearing before any sentence was passed. The 'judge' gave him a chance to explain himself.

'I got the big pocket stitched on the left to cover a tear in the pants,' he said. 'Why is there a big pocket on the right side then?' he was asked. 'For symmetry my Lord, so I look presentable.'

Mr Chadha had had enough by then and he dismissed Rajesh without a scratch on his tender skin. Varun and Sanjay were incensed; not just for the differential treatment, but since the idea of cargoes in school was Rajesh's in the first place.

Rajesh would do his father proud in the future by expanding his law practice manifold.

The Computer Symposium Was Bugged
May 2, 1987

As hosts, Columba's would not claim the team trophy for an inter-school computer symposium. But why was I denied the award for finishing third just because Kanchan Mitra from my school finished first?

In my only public speaking gig in school, I prepared diligently for an event called RUN with the tagline: 'A Race Into the Computer Age.' I spent hours in the British Council Library researching and making multimedia presentations on how computers can change education. I was impressed with my show—except for a sixty second window when I blanked out on stage. I could not speak. I froze. I eventually gathered my wits and resumed but not before the judges docked points.

I was placed fourth when the results came out—missing out on a trophy and certificate. But then one of the students on the organizing team confided that I had finished third but was pushed down because the hosts could not be seen taking two of the three individual prizes on offer.

The whole program was bugged in my opinion, leaving me feeling demoralized and cheated.

'Convicts' Should not be Allowed on Class Trips
May 16, 1987

There should be sign outside section E of eleventh and twelfth to read, 'Hazardous Zone, Keep Away.'

Those with the poorest scores in tenth had to settle for section E. One of the reasons why this bunch fared badly was for their propensity to seek and create trouble. The 'weak-hearted' teachers thus maintained a safe distance from them, limiting their interaction to lectures.

The class thus found themselves in a quandary: a trip to the hill station Mussoorie had been planned, but no teacher was willing to risk their limb and dignity by accompanying them. Without one, it would not be a school sanctioned trip, and most parents would not allow the boys to go.

Eventually, the P.T. instructor Mr 'Bloodif' Sharma was persuaded to play chaperone. More like bribed. He demanded a bottle of rum, Rs 3000 and confirmed room booking to give his consent. In advance. The boys had no choice but to acquiesce.

His wariness was not without justification after what happened with Mr Ram, the crafts teacher, the previous year with a similar band of 'convicts.' He had agreed to escort a group but reached the destination to find no alcohol, no money and no room. He had to fend for himself and would have abandoned the boys but for the fear of losing his job.

The party was last reported sober while still driving on the plains. Most were in varying states of inebriation by the time the bus started winding up the Himalayas, the 'babysitter' included. It was dusk when they checked into the hotel and by nine the management must have been rued taking the booking. The hotel was reduced to a barn where animals had lost their minds, running amok untethered.

Mr Sharma was found wandering for his bed, totally unaware of his surroundings. Instead of his room, he walked into a wardrobe—where two boys locked him. Some started babbling about bringing him out lest he suffocate, but no one was in a state to act rationally. Fortunately, Mr Sharma was found in his bed the following morning, still breathing. He did not die under the students' watch.

The rest of the trip passed in a similar foggy state. Including at the Kempty Falls where Mr Sharma went to frolic in the water with five boys who were willing to go along. It is a wonder the group made it back to Delhi with no one missing, injured or dead.

Decoding Cryptic Messages in Magazines for Hook-Ups!
May 31, 1987

Anuj Devan responded to the veiled advertisements in the soft porn magazine *Debonair* to have sex with a middle-aged woman.

With little to do during the summer holidays, I dropped by at his place where I discovered a stash of *Debonair* magazines. 'How do you get your hands on these,' I asked. 'There is a vendor opposite Sagar Ratna restaurant in Defence Colony; he agrees to sell to us even though we are underage,' Anuj said. He showed me a section where people shared any issues they had and readers could respond. Anuj confided he's been writing back and was surprised to hear back from a middle-aged man. He would invite young boys to his house and watch them have sex with his wife.

'He told you that,' I asked. 'Yeah, and called me over too,' said Anuj.

'And?'

'And what? I obliged. It was fun.'

'Weren't you scared?'

'I wasn't alone.'

'Who else was there?'

'Mohit and Ajit.'

'You are messing with me.'

'Believe it or not, your choice,' said Anuj.

I could not sleep sound for a few days, conjuring up images of what my schoolmates were up to. Would I do it given the chance? I did give it a thought and then told myself emphatically: No way!

Why Does Krishna Pick the Phone When Making Out with a Girl?
June 3, 1987

'Why do always call at the wrong time? There is a girl over me.'

We wanted to borrow some class notes from Krishna Wahi, and Rajesh Bharadwaj called him; only to hear a breathless voice exclaiming about the inappropriateness of the call. Rajesh, the lawyer in making, instantly got into a counterargument.

'How do I know you are with a girl? Do you tell me what's a wrong time? Is any time a wrong time? And why the hell are you picking the phone if you are with a girl?'

Slam. Click.

Desperate Situation Calls for Private Tuitions
July 11, 1987

I was in a bad place. I could not get my head around Physics. I had just about passed the subject in class eleven and the boards would be upon us before we realized it. I was destined for academic oblivion only because I had been forced to elect for science.

In desperation, I signed up for private tuitions by Mr S.P. Sharma, another physics teacher in our school; it was the only time in my life I would take extra classes like these. He lived in a barsaati (top floor apartments with two rooms typically and a large terrace). He took us in groups of four, sitting in a semi-covered verandah. The fee was a small fortune at the time—Rs 400 per student per session. He had students coming till late into the evening, earning him many times over what a teacher's salary was.

Mr Sharma was a Godsend. I managed to score ninety-two in physics in the boards. The high marks were not an indicator of my understanding of the subject but my ability to game the question paper after the tuitions.

Pouring Drinking Water Over Chemistry Class
July 22, 1987

We would do anything to disrupt classes. Even breaking the pot.

We had an earthen pot in our classroom, filled with drinking water. Mrs Behl walked in to find it in pieces with water splashed at the top of the room. The mess would have to be cleared before she could stand there to write on the blackboard and teach us chemistry.

When she asked who did it; Gaurav Narula confessed he did so accidentally. He was sure Rajeev Barua would have snitched on him had he not owned up, revealing it to be a deliberate act. Not only did she not punish him, Mrs Behl commended Gaurav for owning up to what was a mistake. 'We should all learn from Gaurav—it a sign of one's character,' she said. The period was mostly wasted in getting the room in order.

You should have seen Rajeev's expression. He wanted to pour a pot of sulphuric acid on Gaurav's head.

Caught in the Act in a Club
August 5, 1987

Breaking News: One of ours was caught having sex in the bathrooms of Friends Colony Club.

The corridors of St. Columba's were abuzz with shame and scandal. And envy if one were to be honest. Swapan Bahal, our very own Val Kilmer going by looks, was apprehended in the act by the guards of the club. Any attempts to hush the matter came to naught—an alarm was raised, the two teenagers mortified with embarrassment amongst their social circle of South Delhi's elite.

How did word spread around the school so quickly? Because of voyeurs like Rishabh Seth who knew what was happening; along with two others, he had been looking in through the ventilators when the act was on. In fact, they are the ones who were spotted first, leading the guards to the scene of the 'crime.' Even as Swapan and the girl stood crying and pleading, the guys were laughing their heads off at their plight. It did not take long to break the news wherever they found an interested audience.

We would learn such voyeurism was acceptable amongst this set of boys—they would 'peek in' when any were in the act, usually at Mohit's place since his parents were out for work all day. Most of our mothers were housewives, so empty houses were a rarity.

What was our reaction when he heard about the Swapan incident? For sure, no one moralised. We were amused; we had never had anything as juicy to talk about in nearly twelve years in school. There was no sympathy for him either. If anything, we were jealous—this bastard was sexually active while we were dragging our virginity around like an unwieldy rock.

A truth hit home: The 1980s were not as conservative or innocent as we thought them to be. After all there were a bunch of boys who had already crossed the threshold of 'manhood.'

Only Good-Looking Teachers Will Get a Lift
August 11, 1987

'You didn't give a lift to Mrs Raisingh today?'

The history teacher habitually missed her bus and would slip up even more frequently because there was an alternative. Jatinder Sahni used to cross her stop in his car a few minutes after the bus and offer her a lift when she was in distress. But on this day, he did not.

'No, I didn't pick her. She's made a habit of it, so I look the other way when crossing the Moti Bagh bus stop lest she hail me,' he explained. 'Good for the class, they got a free period.'

Of course, if the teacher was a Ms Robinson or a Ms Sandra, Jatinder might have bribed the bus driver to not pick them!

Can Ambition Make Macbeth of Us?
August 17, 1987

'Did you notice the silence in the room whenever death was being depicted on screen?'

Mr Rocha had arranged a viewing of the film adaptation of our prescribed text, *The Tragedy of Macbeth*. 'A hush always descends whenever you are witnessing death,' Mr Rocha pointed out. We may not have realized it while watching the film but agreed with him when we gave it a thought. It has stayed ingrained in me; I tend to observe body language of people when watching death on any screen, even today.

The subject of death led to the cause of violence in the story. Mr Rocha triggered off a debate when he attributed Macbeth's evil streak to ambition. We argued how ambition can't only be a bad thing—but the English teacher stayed adamant on it being a negative trait. Not convincing for twelfth graders on the cusp of pursuing their own ambitions in life.

There could be an explanation for the divergence of views between Mr Rocha and us. Many a teacher may not be subscribing to the idea of ambition as others do. For they may be seeking contentment in their occupation, and all things simple and beautiful.

Do Any Teachers Sleep with the Boys?
September 12, 1987

There were rumours of Ms Kritika Sanyal being involved with Krishna Wahi. But there was no proof till Badal walked into Krishna's bedroom.

Those were the days when you did not necessarily call before going to someone's house. We were lesser likely to as students, roaming about town, with no telephone connectivity. In fact, you could literally walk into each other's homes without even ringing the bell—front doors and gates were not kept as secured as they are now.

There was thus nothing abnormal about Badal walking into Krishna's bedroom without announcing his presence. He was not expecting to find Ms Sanyal propped up against the head of the bed, Krishna on the floor by her side. What was Badal's reaction? He just smirked at the teacher, as if to tell her the cat's out of the bag. Surprisingly, neither of them requested Badal to keep him mouth shut.

Badal being Badal, he let half the school know. He still did not have definite proof of any sexual relationship between the two, but he painted a picture others wanted to see. Some defended Krishna, saying Ms Sanyal was being paid by his father for private tuitions, and they could well have been chatting casually. In the fog of such stories, you believed what you wanted to.

On her part, Ms Sanyal gave Badal hell in the classroom: ticking him off for the slightest mistake, penalising his papers as harshly as she could. Badal is not the kind to care for such trifles. Then, and now.

A Suggestion: Don't Plant Diwali Bombs in School
October 5, 1987

The week started with a bang—literally.

Sanuj Nath planted a Diwali bomb in the suggestions box below the principal's office. And it went off as timed. Br Noronha was probably the most tolerant of principals we have had but there was no forgiving this act. Sanuj was rusticated with immediate effect. He would have to enrol in some lowly school to be eligible to appear in the boards. After over twelve years in the school, his idiocy denied him the honour of graduating from St. Columba's School.

Who Will Marry a Woman Not a Virgin?
October 19, 1987

'How many of you are agreeable to marrying a woman who is not a virgin?'

Mr Rocha asked this question out of the blue, offering no context or rationale. Only three hands in a class of fifty went up. Not surprising considering prevalent views and conditioning of society at the time. Every boy fantasised or even indulged in sex, but the woman they married had to be 'pure.'

Had he regrouped the class ten years later, I am sure the response would have been very different.

I Am an Intelligent Boy Who Has Yet to Realise His Potential
November 2, 1987

'If you hit a teacher, you will not be issued a Character Certificate and thus be denied admission to any university.'

Mr Chadha burst out when a third pellet hit him while writing on the blackboard, back to the class. The 'shooter' was Sanjay Sharma, known as 'Slingshot Cowboy', for his expertise in using rubber bands to launch paper 'bullets' to strike victims accurately over long distances. Mr Chadha was already on a short fuse, having been hit by a student a few days ago; no one would confirm if it happened or who the boy was, but it was believed to be true.

Each of us were issued a Character Certificate upon completion of school. We were rated for our performance in academics, sports and extra-curriculars, and for traits like Leadership, Maturity, Initiative, Concern for Others and Respect by Faculty and by Peers. I would score Excellent in all except sports where it was average; there was no basis for judging me on extra-curriculars. The subjective remark by Mr Peter Rocha for me: 'An intelligent boy who has yet to realise his potential.'

Despite the importance Mr Chadha was giving the Character Certificate, no university requisitioned it when evaluating our admission applications.

We Rejoiced Pakistan's Loss, And Mourned Ours
November 5, 1987

India's honeymoon run came to an agonising end when we lost to England in the semi-finals of the Reliance Cup 1987 to decide the world champions. We had won major trophies since our victory in the previous edition in 1983 and the loss was no less an upset than when we defeated England at the same stage four years ago.

It was quite a humbling day for a nation who had celebrated Pakistan's defeat to Australia the previous day in Lahore; the latter would become the dark horses who went on to lift the trophy just like India. My father chided me when I said it was more important Pakistan lost than India's win. I will not forget his look when we were eliminated.

It would turn out to be Sunil Gavaskar's last outing for the country, having broken all major batting records by the time he retired. Earlier in the year, he became the first batsman to cross 10,000 runs in test cricket. There were accusations of him throwing his wicket away against England to spite his captain, Kapil Dev—unfair, with no basis, for someone who took everything that bowlers sent his way for sixteen years. Gavaskar's legacy was too deeply etched for any controversies to wipe away.

What seemed a footnote was a harbinger of things to come: The Reliance group, an Indian business conglomerate, sponsored the world cup for what was an unprecedented deal in Indian sports. As the Indian economy opened in the coming years, investments by Indian brands would change the politics and economics of cricket globally.

Who Can Swear the Dirtiest?
November 13, 1987

The last of our annual picnics was coming to an end—a tradition we came to look forward to in every class. On the way back from Suraj Kund, someone proposed we mark the occasion with a competition to see who could swear the filthiest. The cue was barely given when a shouting match started, each trying to outdo the other in profanities. Every possible cuss word we had heard in our lives echoed in the bus.

If there was an award for the most imaginative, it would go to Manav Abrol for: *'Chipkali ki gaand pe paseene ki boond* (A drop of sweat on the ass of a lizard).'

Of All the People, the Shoe Hit Mrs Rebello!
November 24, 1987

Varun Pawha threw a shoe at Rajesh Bharadwaj, who ducked in time. It maintained its flight path, crossed the window and crash landed, hitting Mrs Rebello's shoulder. Of all the faculty, the shoe had to find the most volatile of them all.

She spotted the offender through the window, guilt and fear all over his face. She walked in and dragged him by the ear to the principal's office. Rajesh followed, hobbling, wearing only one shoe. 'Ma'am, could you give me the shoe, our cricket match is starting soon,' requested Rajesh.

'No, I will not,' she screamed. 'THIS IS EVIDENCE!'

Rajesh had to wait half an hour for the shoe to be returned, making it to the field just in time before his name was scratched from the line-up. Varun got away with just a verbal rap on his knuckles after he apologised. He was fortunate the new principal, Br Noronha, was not very trigger happy with Charlie. A sign of changes coming soon.

In any case, within a few weeks, we would be over with classes in the school. I am sure no teacher wanted any sour memories of our last days. And I can bet Br Noronha was amused at the incident even though he could not show it.

It's Farewell to Us

January 28, 1988

As our librarian Mrs Mohinder would say: 'Time is over!'

Yes, it was time for us to leave St. Columba's School. Class eleven stepped up to give us an honourable and emotional farewell. Over lunch as was now the norm.

We passed the lamp, symbolic of the passage of leadership, to our immediate juniors. A few of us delivered short speeches, triggering tears in those on stage and in the audience. We stood in front of the Junior School building, where we entered as five-year-olds and leaving soon at eighteen. No institution can be as life impacting as being in one through this age range.

On the fun side, we were awarded merit certificates for achievements like sporting the longest locks or being the quietest one. A band came on, belting western numbers—we danced to the music, not caring about the dust on our shoes and suits in the open field. It was one of those afternoons we wished the music would never stop.

It was the afternoon when we wished to stay boys forever.

Rohit Vaid was going around humming this song in a loop, reminiscing about a future yet to show its face:

Jab hum jawaan honge,
Jaane kahan honge ...

When we become the youth, wonder where we will be ... and so went the song. From the 1983 movie *Betaab*, it also marked the Bollywood debut of two youths Sunny Deol and Amrita Singh who would go on to have successful acting careers. At least they got the answer to where they will be. Rohit was making it sound like a spoof, not caring where we would be. Incidentally, he would become a filmmaker!

Why Would Taj Mahal Hotel Fuss Over One Milkshake?
January 28, 1988

'Someone has to pay for the milkshake, or the rest will not be allowed to leave.'

Our farewell party got over by four in the afternoon and no one was keen to go home. We realized we may not be dressed to kill but we certainly were to go to a five-star hotel. So, a score of us trooped our way to Machan, the coffee shop at Taj Mahal hotel.

We could only afford to order a milkshake each, even that being an indulgence for some. But heck, you finish school only once. We spent over two hours finishing them, sucking every last drop from the bottom and sides of the glasses, getting increasingly boisterous as the evening set in.

The celebrations had to conclude eventually, so we paid for our drinks and set out to leave. But were stopped by the staff. They had not received payment for one milkshake. We had no clue who left without paying, but the rest of us were expected to on his behalf. We refused. Arguments ensued. We were in no rush; we could wait it out. Eventually the other side blinked and we were allowed to go.

All this pow-wow over one piddly milkshake?

Merwyn Fernandes Bid Us Farewell Too

It had to be a Guinness record!

Merwyn Fernandes entered school in 1975 with us. While all of us left in 1988, he stayed on. As a computer teacher initially, been given the additional responsibility for Physical Education later. He pursued a college degree via correspondence. When I met him while writing this memoir, he was still in the school, fifty years after he was first admitted to it. He will retire at sixty as per rules.

He would thus have the unique distinction of being in the same institution all his academic and professional life. He has not known a world outside St. Columba's. Isn't that something? Can be a matter of envy too if you love your school enough.

So, when we were given a farewell by eleventh graders, Merwyn got one too—but he also gave his batchmates one. Telling them to come back anytime and he will be there to greet us!

When Ninety-Nine Equals 100 in Maths
May 9, 1988

I did it! I finally scored a hundred in mathematics. That too in the most important exams for a student in India: the class twelve boards.

Yet the certificate read ninety-nine. Why? No one is perfect, according to the ISCE board. I would spend the rest of my life explaining I did not lose a mark, they took it away. And ninety-nine equals one hundred for ICSE's mathematicians.

All through my school years, my grandfather and father wanted to see me score a hundred in maths. I finally did—and I cried for my grandfather, who was no longer around to savour the moment. If only he had lived nine months longer.

1988: A New India as We Step Out of Our Comfort Zones

It may be a coincidence or maybe it was our destiny: a very different India took shape at the same time we got out of the comfort zones of school and home, to being out in the wild. First in university and then into the working world.

Viswanathan Anand, exactly two days older to me, became the first Indian chess Grandmaster around the time I was all nerves preparing for my class twelve boards. Another Sagittarian, legendary actor and filmmaker Raj Kapoor died at the relatively young age of sixty-three. Palika Bazaar, the underground market in Connaught Place selling everything spurious and genuine, was flooded with sets of VHS tapes of his movies. I was tempted to buy one box but was not given the money for it.

Normalcy and peace would finally be restored to the state of Punjab with Operation Black Thunder was widely seen as a turning point in curbing separatism in Punjab.. Rajiv Gandhi brought down the voting age from twenty-one to eighteen, making millions more eligible to have a say on who will govern us. Including us.

More significantly, the former defence minister V.P. Singh formed a new political party, the Janata Dal. While he was voted to power the following year for his anti-corruption stance, this issue would take a backseat when he implemented the recommendations of the Mandal Commission. Henceforth, jobs in the government would also be reserved for OBCs, or Other Backward Classes, in addition to reservations for Scheduled Castes and Tribes.

People on either side of the divide took to the streets, some to protest, others to block the protestors. On September 19, 1990, Rajiv Goswami survived a self-immolation bid as a mark of protest but suffered severe burns. Some claimed it was the mob that set him on fire, passing it off as a suicide bid. During this time, I launched an activist magazine, *Youth Marg*, with other college students, covering the protests in depth besides other issues, but we could not sustain it beyond one edition.

Of course, as with the first non-Congress Government in the late 1970s, this one would collapse before its term of five years. The Parliament would be dissolved in 1991; Rajiv Gandhi was predicted to return to power and probably would have, had he not been assassinated on May 21, 1991, while on the campaign trail. Congress would win, the new prime Minister P.V. Narasimha Rao and his able finance minister Manmohan Singh liberalised the economy, unleashing wealth creation opportunities not possible with the earlier mindset of government controls.

Our generation would enter the workforce just as the new policies would kick in. Opening pathways even the most optimistic of Indians would not have dreamt of.

You Laugh Differently with Those You Have Grown Up With

There is a difference in friends you make during adulthood and mates you evolved with in classrooms.

There was a lull in interactions for a few years after we finished school. We went our different ways; higher education and careers dispersed us geographically. We had houses and homes to build. We remained close within our cliques, but the larger regrouping happened over two decades later. Long enough for some athletes to be paunchy, some debaters hesitant, some stars dimmed. But also, for laggards to be winning races, for those in the shadows to be standing in the sun, for those who looked up to others to be heroes themselves. The wild and the ruffian had been tamed, the docile were now heavy weights in their own right. The bright kept their date with destiny, charting impressive professional progress. Of course, there were those like the doggy's tail: exactly as they were.

But we reconnected. Like we did annually after summer vacations. Twenty years and more seemed no longer than the seven-week break. We just eased into each other's company, our guards down, not needing to make any impressions. School was the leveller for us from varied backgrounds and the passage of life did not change that.

We met like brothers. With kindness. We laughed as we always did. With no reason, at poor jokes, at witty ones. We could mock each other's appearance, we could abuse without provocation and not cause any offence. Because we never had any egos, any pride, any envy with each other. Because you don't have these emotions at five, or six, or seven. That's how we stayed with each other as we got older in school and aged in life. Such has been the natural state of being with one another then and always.

Because, without realizing or articulating it, we were and are a family; agnostic of religion, financial worth, social status, professional achievements and sense of humour.

Trivia, Stickies, Quotes & Anecdotes

Before I sign off, here is a random collection of stuff worth mentioning …

The School Address

The original name and address of the school was: St. Columba's High School, Alexandra Place, New Delhi. It is now St. Columba's School, 1 Ashoka Place, New Delhi 110001.

The Boys Loved Detention

Br D'Souza introduced detention in his last year in the school. It backfired because no one minded it—gave them a reason to be out of their homes.

Swinging Tie with a Battery In It

'Pritash Mathur taught me how to fight with a tie in class one. He shoved a battery in each of our ties and swung wildly. Fortunately, we did not hit the other. Unfortunately, the headmaster Br McPhilmey spotted us. We ran. But I was identified because of my blond hair.' – DJ Singh

Brooke Bond

A joke published in the school mag 1981-82: Why didn't Brooke Shields marry James Bond? Because she didn't want to be called Brooke Bond.

Flower Polish

Our uniform included black leather shoes—polished. There were times when we reached school in dirty shoes. The only solution? Pick a silk cotton flower found on the ground in abundance, use it as a brush with the nectar providing the gloss. It worked only during the flowering season though.

Walter of the Gong

Walter, the one with a gentle face, greying hair, and slim frame was responsible for ringing the bell in the Middle School. It was a gong that would be struck multiple times for the whole school to hear. Even if you missed it, the sight of scurrying boys would tell you Walter just did his job.

Checking if Brother Really Buried

It seems many a lady teacher and mother of boys would swoon at the sight of Br McPhilmey. The boys would too—but from the whacks they got. When he passed away, some claimed to have attended his funeral service only to see him buried with their own eyes—and feel safe.

Brothers are Forbidden Fruit

Br Pinto once spoke about how teachers would pull his leg about being besieged by pretty young mothers. Brothers in general were charming, no doubt, and their celibate status probably made the 'forbidden fruit' even more desirable.

Here's to You. Ms Robinson …

Everyone had a crush on Ms Robinson, who was not much older than the Senior School boys. The computer teacher, Mr Shahid Ali Khan, was quite indiscreet in his admiration of her but had the sense to maintain a safe distance to avoid any awkward situations.

High on Lab Alcohol

One of the attendants in the Middle School chemistry lab seemed to be in a continual state of high—by toasting with alcohol, meant for experiments. Everyone believed it, but it was unlikely the lab alcohol was suitable for human consumption.

Unnecessary Scolding at Home

It was the norm to have our parents sign all class test papers; these did not count towards our mid-term and final exams but kept us on our toes. Usually, we scored lower in these than in our exams because we did not take them seriously. But getting signed meant being scolded all year round unnecessarily. Why couldn't they just limit it to twice a year after the two main exams?

How Do You Clean a Rubber?

Ms Gill showed me how to clean a rubber when it was dirty after use. Ok, the eraser as it is now known. Take a rag and rub against it to reveal the whiteness. In the absence of any piece of cloth, I would use the sides of my trousers. So, I always have a clean rubber when required.

'See Me'—The Words We Dreaded

It was common to see teachers walk through the gates with a jute or canvas bag heavily laden with notebooks for correction, brought back the following morning without fail. Each meticulously checked and with remarks added when necessary. 'Good', 'Fair', 'Could do better' allowed our breathing to stay normal. However, the seemingly innocuous 'See me' held a completely different and dreaded connotation!

Speaking Into the Earpiece to Save 50 p

We had a telephone in the foyer of the Middle School; local calls could be made by dropping a 50 p coin in it. It was referred to as PCO or Public Call Office. The coin had to be dropped only after you heard a response from the other end. Someone came up with a theory that the calling party could hear you if you shouted loud enough into the earpiece; we tried to save money with this approach. We believed our parents had heard we would be late reaching home but they had not. Faith in the instrument was anyway low as calls might not get through even after dropping the money—there was no system of a refund so why risk it?

When 'Friends' Got It Right

A scene from the popular television series, *Friends*, hit a Columban's woes right on the spot:

Julia Roberts (in a special appearance) to Chandler Bing (played by late Matthew Perry) in a bar: How come all I can think about is putting that ice in my mouth and licking you … all over?

Chandler (after a thoughtful pause): Because I went to an all-boys high school and God is making up for it?

Vocabulary

How implied meanings and thus usage of words and phrases changed over time …

Gay was happy back then.

We drew and fabricated a **Weather Cock** in class, but now kids draw a Weathervane or Wind Vane.

Text was a noun. Now it is popularly used as a verb.

'**How now, brown cow**' was an informal greeting, confined to the deepest recesses of memory now.

Passings

Ms Gill and Mrs Vaid, our class teachers in sixth and seventh respectively, would both pass at relatively young ages a few years after we graduated from Columba's. Cancer would take away two of the finest teachers out there. Ms Gill had got married to Mr Burrett, our Geography teacher, who moved to Doon School when we were in the tenth. Mrs Vaid's son was our batchmate. Uncanny when you think about how two teachers in successive grades passed away in the manner they did.

Shortly after we finished school, Pankaj Kanodia would shoot himself. We will never know why. The lexicon of the time had only one word for it: depression. My memories of him were more from the final two years—he would worry about his batting and wanted to understand how I shave clean around my chin.

The Layout of the School

The school had three primary blocks in our time. In the middle stood the Senior School for classes eleven and twelve, administration and accounts, the principal's office and residential rooms for Brothers. On either side of this building were the Middle School and the Junior School. The former had classes four to ten, the latter kindergarten to third. Two sections of fourth are housed in the Junior School.

There are two fields separating the three buildings. The main canteen is in the Middle School, with the other two having kiosks selling food and beverages. The swimming pool is at one end, behind the Junior School.

A fourth block came up later, with a multipurpose indoor sports and gymnasium facility, and accommodations for Brothers.

The all-girls Convent of Jesus and Mary School stands adjacent to ours, separated by a common wall. Between the two is the Sacred Heart Cathedral, one of the most important places of worship for Christians.

GLOSSARY

BOARDS
Exams you take at the end of grades ten and twelve. There are different education boards who conduct these and hence the name. St. Columba's was affiliated to what was commonly referred to as ICSE, but its actual name was the **Council for the Indian School Certificate Examinations**. The certificates that we were awarded read **Indian Certificate of Secondary Education Examination** (hence ICSE) in class ten, and **Indian School Certificate (Year-12) Examination** in the twelfth.

BREAK
The mid-morning break between classes, lasting about half an hour.

BROTHER
Those belonging to the **Congregation of Christian Brothers,** founded by Edmund Rice (who would later be known as Br Ignatius) in 1820 in Ireland. The book refers to them as Brother (with a capital B) or Br, not to be confused with brothers (that we boys were) and our brotherhood.

COPY
The notebooks we wrote in.

CANTEEN
The cafeteria.

CLASS
Referred to as Standards or Grades in many places. We had class one, two, three and so on till twelfth. Our **Section** could also be referred to as our **Class.** We could thus be class twelve, or we would refer to 12A as our class.

CLASS TEACHER
Each section was assigned a teacher who would manage everything about their class, including filling out and distributing Report Cards. They were the primary point of contact for parents. They would usually teach one subject in senior classes, but even two or three in junior and middle classes. They also sat or stood in the centre of the first row of the annual class photo.

CLASS TEST
A tool to torture us, these were mini exams during the term. Marks in these did not count towards your term results—we would not take these seriously and score below our capabilities. Papers were sent home to be signed by parents, unnecessarily causing their blood pressure to fluctuate.

CJM
Convent of Jesus & Mary, supposedly the 'sister' school adjoining ours.

DTC
Delhi Transport Corporation, a state run bus transport utility serving New Delhi. Their buses were contracted to ferry us to and from home. Routes were numbered Z1, Z2 and so on.

EXAMS
Tests conducted at the end of each **Term.**

EXTRA-CURRICULARS
Any activity other than academics and sports. Would including quizzing, debating, theatre, music, singing and elocution.

INTER-CLASS
Usually referred to competitions between **Sections** of the same **Class**. It could thus be a football match between 5-A and 5-C. Any competition between grades, say seventh vs eighth, was unheard of.

MARKS
The grades or scores we received.

PARENT TEACHER MEETING
The day when parents were called to school to meet teachers, collect Report Cards and discuss their son's progress.

PENCIL BOX
The box or pouch we carried our stationery in.

PERIOD
A school day was divided into eight sessions called periods. Sex education classes taught us what it is for women, and that there was nothing dirty or inauspicious about it.

P.T.
Physical Training, what is mostly known as Physical Education. We had one or two periods a week for P.T.

PICNIC
An annual outing to a landmark park, lake or monument in the Delhi area. We left school early morning, back in time to catch the afternoon bus back home. Everyone brought food to share and games to play. Each section had its own separately. Teachers had to accompany the boys as a rule.

PRACTICALS
Laboratory work and exams for Physics, Biology and Chemistry.

REPORT CARD
A record of our marks in exams and of our conduct. Parents had to collect these in person at the end of exams, and sign the same too.

RUBBER
Object used to erase a mistake (not to avoid committing one in the first place). Now kids would be slapped for asking for a 'rubber'.

RULER
The measuring scale; came in two sizes – six and twelve inches long. The latter was also called footruler (gap between foot and ruler is deliberately missed). The wooden ones were also a weapon in hands of staff and the plastic one could also be used to measure certain parts of the anatomy as we grew (pun intended).

SECTION
Each class or grade was divided into five sections: A, B, C, D and E. Most stayed in the same section from Kindergarten to tenth. I was thus in KG-D, 1-D, 2-D, and so on.

STAY BACK
Be in school after regular hours. Since scheduled school bus service would be over, we had to find our own way back home.

SWORD OF HONOUR
Awarded to one student in the graduating class twelve for overall performance in sports, academics and extra-curriculars.

TERM
School year was initially divided into three terms and later into two—each culminating into exams. The syllabus was for the whole year, not the term.

TIFFIN
The lunch we carried from home. The container was called Tiffin Box.

WATER BOTTLE
The bottle we carried drinking water in. A few carried insulated flasks to keep water cool, but most could not afford them. In any case, the ones at that time broke on the inside on impact; unbreakable ones came in much later.

A Little Boy's Future. A Man's Past. The Same Story. Irrevocable.

14 November 1975/14 November 2025

'Did you take good care of me?'

It's a five-year-old boy asking me. Correction: It's *the* five-year-old boy asking me. We are in a café, him slurping a cold coffee, me sipping an Americano. He is digging into my tea cake, a liberty no one has ever been allowed. I am possessive about my cake and popcorn. But this kid can get away with it. Because he is not a kid, he is *the* kid. He is *me*.

He has invited me actually, to ask how life panned out. He wants to be sure I will be a suitable caretaker, not that he has a choice. But he wants the assurance. He takes his mouth away from the straw, gives me that interrogating look—expecting me to do the talking, not waiting for prompts. Just spill the beans about what the future holds for him. A future now, my past, irrevocable.

The first few years after school will be a bore, a decade spent dragging my feet. Studying engineering, building computers—choices thrust upon me. A few years of sports management promised to get adrenalin pumping, only if others had not played foul and the referee not taken sides. Despair would send me back to school, to study journalism and photography. That is when I would start living, making up for lost time.

Newspapers taught me how to craft stories and I would use the skill acquired to write my books. As a travel writer first, taking me everywhere, showing me life from different vantage points. Shaping my thinking, my psyche, the caterpillar undergoing metamorphosis for a butterfly to emerge. I would out-evolve old friends, synthesising under the light shed by new.

There would be stumbles, there would be mistakes. The heart would break, but the heart would heal too, in anticipation of love. The romantic kind everyone dreams of and for a life, few spare a thought to.

I look at the boy, who has not blinked while I speak. I smile.

'I will give you one hell of a ride kiddo, the kind no one in our batch will. For a while, it will seem they have sprinted ahead, but we will never be bothered about catching up. We will chart our own course, live our own adventures. While others climb hills, we will seek mountains. Not to stand atop others, but to touch the heavens and skies. While others conform, we will define. While others accumulate burdens, we will shed. Others will compare; we will not be bothered.

'We will fall, we will stumble, we will hurt, we will cry. But we will keep going. Never losing our cheer, our hope, our optimism. Always experimenting, always creating. We will paint masterpieces to please the galleries and we will doodle to please our whims. We will be the outliers, standing in the middle.

'We will be prepared well for life. After all, we are Charlie's Boys.'

For more anecdotes, photos and videos of Charlie's Boys, visit https://ajayjain.com/charlies-boys

HarperCollins *Publishers* India

At HarperCollins India, we believe in telling the best stories and finding the widest readership for our books in every format possible. We started publishing in 1992; a great deal has changed since then, but what has remained constant is the passion with which our authors write their books, the love with which readers receive them, and the sheer joy and excitement that we as publishers feel in being a part of the publishing process.

Over the years, we've had the pleasure of publishing some of the finest writing from the subcontinent and around the world, including several award-winning titles and some of the biggest bestsellers in India's publishing history. But nothing has meant more to us than the fact that millions of people have read the books we published, and that somewhere, a book of ours might have made a difference.

As we look to the future, we go back to that one word—a word which has been a driving force for us all these years.

Read.